SHADOWS OF PAIN

SHADOWS OF PAIN

Intimacy and Sexual Problems in Family Life

Vimala Pillari, DSW, LCSW

JASON ARONSON INC.
Northvale, New Jersey
London

This book was set in 11 pt. New Aster by Alabama Book Composition of Deatsville, Alabama and printed and bound by Book-mart Press of North Bergen, New Jersey.

10 9 8 7 6 5 4 3 2 1

Library of Congress Cataloging-in-Publication Data

Pillari, Vimala.
Shadows of pain : intimacy and sexual problems in family life / by Vimala Pillari.
p. cm.
Includes bibliographical references and index.
ISBN 0-7657-0009-3 (alk. paper)
1. Family—Psychological aspects. 2. Intimacy (Psychology).
3. Psychosexual development. 4. Sex (Psychology). 5. Interpersonal relations. 6. Family—Mental health. I. Title.
RC488.5.P555 1996
616.89—dc20 96-14384

Manufactured in the United States of America. Jason Aronson Inc. offers books and cassettes. For information and catalog write to Jason Aronson Inc., 230 Livingston Street, Northvale, New Jersey 07647.

Dedicated with love
to my husband,
Steve Lassiter

Contents

Acknowledgments

It is time to say thanks to those who have enriched me in my heart and helped in the process of writing this book. To my clients, from whom I learn a great deal every day, and without whose wholehearted presentation of issues and problems I could not have gotten into the intricacies of intimacy.

To those who helped me unwaveringly in this project: Dr. Lyman Wynne from the University of Rochester, who shared his ideas of intimacy and pseudomutuality; Margaret Manzella, professor at the University of Buffalo at New York, a well-known sex therapist; and Dr. Moses Newsome, Dean, Norfolk State University, for his constant, unwavering support. Thanks to Dr. Isaac Alcabes for his complete and caring support, intellectual stimulation, and constructive criticism, and to my special colleagues, Dr. Charles Broadfield of Virginia, Dorothy Sawyer of Florida, and Dr. Gene Gibbons and Dr. Shirley Cox from Brigham Young University for their support and encouragement.

At Jason Aronson Inc. my special thanks to Michael Moskowitz, Norma Pomerantz, who was always available for queries and emergencies, and M'lou Pinkham, my editor. As the editing progressed, my relationship with M'lou Pinkham changed from quiet reserve to one of complete enjoyment as she sprinkled the hard work of editing with humor and joviality. Her dedicated and thorough editing is greatly appreciated.

Finally, my special thanks to my son, Kapil. To my husband, Steve, who calls himself my co-sufferer in thinking and writing as I go through the process, how do I say thanks? I don't know—so I dedicate this book to him!

CHAPTER ONE

Interrelationship of Sexual and Relationship Difficulties

RYAN IS A FOOTBALL coach. As a football coach, he has given himself permission to get worked up, laugh, shout, and cry with his team, but he would have a harder time expressing what he feels outside of his coaching role.

Who is Ryan? Ryan grew up in a family where they were not allowed to discuss feelings, because "feelings were not important." When he was 10 years old, he went away with his best friend, Peter, and his family for a weekend at the beach. Ryan saw that his friend's parents behaved very differently from his own. They laughed, they cried, and they talked freely to each other. Ryan was surprised that when his friend fell down, slipped and hurt himself, and fought to hold back his tears, his parents were very supportive, encouraging him to say what he felt and reassuring him that it was all right to cry.

Ryan thought he was experiencing the best moments of his young life. He realized that his own parents handled matters very differently—it *was* all right to cry and talk about feelings. It took Ryan a long time to learn how to express feelings, but it was easy to do in sports. Intimacy had been neglected in his own family, and Ryan had problems with relationships, particularly with women, because he did not know how to be close without "doing things."

Six-year-old Amy was playing on the school grounds with other children while the teacher supervised the games. Unlike other children, Amy was talkative, and surprised the teacher by her affectionate ways as well as her adult language. When the teacher asked her, "Where did you learn to speak like that?" Amy replied, "I want to tell you a secret." The next day, when no other children were present, Amy said to the teacher: "I'm going to tell you a secret my Daddy and I have. It is a secret game—I touch Daddy's big 'pee-wee' and he touches me . . . down here. I feel funny when I touch Daddy but it feels good for me. You are my favorite teacher and I want you to know all my secrets, but please don't tell anyone."

The little girl was being molested by her stepfather and the teacher discussed it with the school counselor. After preliminary sessions with Amy, the matter was reported, as required, to Protective Services.

What was the history in Amy's home? Amy's mother had been divorced twice and the third man she married, Rick, was an alcoholic, although both she and Rick claimed that he "drinks just a little." Amy's mother worked two jobs and was not at home most of the day and part of the night. She was shocked to hear about the abuse, and angry, because she had trusted her husband. Rick came from a family in which he had been sexually abused by his stepfather and later by his older brother and sisters. He was repeating the pattern by abusing his stepdaughter, but also drowning his own problems and pain by drinking. He and his wife did not have the foggiest idea about how to be intimate.

Lionel too had difficulty in relationships with women. If he got close to a woman and wanted to marry her, he would panic and run without knowing why. His mother would talk about it forever.

Lionel is an only son and does not have a father. He says that his mother is obsessed with his getting married. Although she seems to have friends of her own, she is always worrying about Lionel's love life. She constantly tells him that she lives for his happiness. He feels smothered by her; when he dates anyone, she is very interested in knowing all the details, about the girl's family history and anything else she can get out of him. He is upset because he feels that she is "really stuck on me, like a leech."

This is an example of *fusion*. His mother has no life of her own. She is totally enmeshed with her son and sees him as an extension of herself. Although he is lonely and wants a family, he rebels against her by not getting married. He said in therapy, "I do not wish to please her." What Lionel needs to know is that he has to live his life for himself and fulfill his own desires and understand his self-defeating behaviors. His rebellion against his mother is a reaction to years of total control by her. The constant bickering between the two has left him weak and numb in his relationships with women.

Sexual problems in family life have multiple sources that are closely interconnected to intimacy and relationship problems. In Ryan's family it is "facts and no feelings" relationships, in which activities are substituted for talking and sharing. How could Ryan develop an intimate relationship with another human being? In Amy's case the intergenerational patterns of sexual abuse affect her relationship with her stepfather. Why would the mother choose such a man? What about her own relationship issues? In Lionel's family it is a smothering, overwhelming relationship between mother and son. Overinvolvement with children is also a symptom of poor adult relationships.

In all these relationships there are symptoms of pain, hurt, and anger. Often they are the shadows of pain from the family of origin. Sexuality and intimacy are interrelated. Learning about sexuality and emotions never occurs in a vacuum. Every experience becomes a part of the background against which new learning takes place.

As Lively and Lively (1991) indicate, *sexuality* (in the broadest sense) encompasses an individual's personal growth in all its dimensions, including how a person relates to others. We are sexual beings, and sexuality does not just mean *what we do*, it is *what we are.* We develop an identity, male or female, in terms of behavior that is masculine or feminine. All of us have our own unique sexuality. Physiological, social, cultural, biological, and emotional forces contribute to make us the sexual beings we are. We are conditioned from birth based upon biological and genetic factors, and this is a continuing process until we die.

Lively and Lively (1991) also say that sexuality includes the biological nature of a person, the physical aspects of sexual relations, and the many other aspects of sex-linked behaviors. It is not purely physical, as projected by today's mass media, which often distort sexuality, focusing on the genitalia and sexual responses rather than on sensual expression involving the whole personality and relationships with others. The goals of human sexuality are more than attainment of sexual gratification through sex or other kinds of stimulation.

The ultimate goal is the integration of our concept of ourselves, our behaviors, our culture, and our value system in interaction with other people. When we develop sexuality in an integrated way, we are capable of developing meaningful relationships with other people, relationships that are attainable and obtainable during each stage of our lives.

An important aspect of sexuality is *intimacy*, feelings involving another person to create a sense of togetherness. Intimacy may be described as a subjective relational experience in which the core components are trusting self-disclosure and a response of communicated empathy (Wynne and Wynne 1986). It is also important to realize that self-disclosure does not necessarily mean intimacy. For example, a divorcing couple who use self-disclosure to "prove" how little they care for one another is not showing intimacy. A key component of intimacy is the willingness to share, verbally and nonverbally, personal feelings, fantasies, and emotionally meaningful experiences and actions, positive and negative, with the expectation and trust that the other person will emotionally comprehend and accept what has been revealed and will not betray or exploit this trust.

In my view of intimacy, an intimate experience has not happened until there is empathetic feedback, that is, until acceptance and acknowledgment are communicated, verbally or nonverbally, as an indication that this trust is justified. In genuine intimacy there is genuine mutuality. In genuine mutuality family members care about each other and wish to connect with each other in real and caring ways. Mutuality deals with the process of long-term relational renewal and re-engagement (Wynne and Wynne 1986). In mutuality there is a shared commitment to one another to shape the relationship as the life cycle unfolds, as new and unexpected events take place, as new interests and aspirations emerge. Mutuality optimizes the likelihood of intimacy. In mutuality the relationship is reshaped multidimensionally, sometimes drastically reorganized, but with continuity of contributions from each person in the relationship.

There are families who come into therapy because they are in a transitional situation in their lives, with divergence, conflict, and changes due to growth and maturation. These may generate many outcomes for relational systems other than mutuality. Without a desire for reengagement such relationships are often discarded with no exploration of reengagement at a different level. For example, Danny and Dottie moved to a new community when Danny received a promotion in his company. Dottie, a professional in her own right, was thrilled at first but very unhappy that she did not find a new job. After three months of fruitless searching and a great deal of discomfort caused by her husband's sarcastic comments about her inability to get a job, Dottie ended up having an affair. Instead of beginning a new life together, Dottie and Danny angrily parted ways, their dreams shattered by the affair. Enduring relationships between partners go beyond sexuality, and require periodic stocktaking, with both people taking into account their own and their partner's needs and preferences, and the quality of what goes on between them.

Environmental forces also influence sexuality and intimacy. They include influences exerted by parents, other adults, and peer groups as well as religious sources and the media. Sexuality (and other aspects of a person's emotionality) and interpersonal relations are interwoven. If children have experienced normal sexual development, they are better equipped to handle sexuality as adults. However, if they are misused sexually as children they may grow up with inappropriate emotional attitudes affecting their psychosocial development. Inappropriate emotions, when rampant, can result in the loss of human warmth and involvement (Gadpaille 1975).

Intimacy occurs in different types of relationships. In caring parent–child relationships, give and take, good communication skills, and the freedom to express feelings are present. There is psychological intimacy and open communication between siblings, relatives, and good friends. Intimacy is not tied only to spousal or partner relationships. A couple's constructive, intimate relationship can lead to proper nurturing of children and respect for their rights, which in turn will produce well-nourished and nurtured adults who are capable of developing meaningful relationships with others.

SYSTEMS APPROACH AS A FRAMEWORK

The basic premise of the systems approach is that in every aspect of our lives all elements are interrelated. An individual's life is woven into a web of mutual human relationships. Transactions between parents and children affect both, and out of these experiences people learn coping and adapting capabilities. Children soak up what they see, hear, and experience. They watch—and listen to—their parents, and imitate their behavior. Unlike adults, they have few outside contacts to fall back on, and they accept whatever is told them as truth.

Kasha was told that bad men wear black coats and one would carry her away; this made such an impression on her that she developed a tremendous fear of men in black coats or jackets. Though the reasons were long forgotten, when Kasha's boyfriend wore a black jacket one evening, it threw her off balance. After some time in therapy, she understood that her irrational fears stemmed from early childhood. Things that children learn about themselves at home become universal truths in their minds.

In family systems we are closely linked to each other. We talk, cry, fight, love, and learn within our families. The parental subsystem has a powerful influence on children. Parents who separate emotionally from each other may form an unhealthy alliance with a child who is used to satisfy the needs of one of the parents.

> Twenty-seven-year-old Lola said in therapy that she used to file her father's fingernails from the time she was 5 years old. To the question, "Why did you do it?" she looked surprised and replied, "Because he wanted me to."
>
> "How about your mother?"
>
> "She was always working, and Mom and Dad used to fight a lot." Lola loved her father. He always called her his "little princess."
>
> "What did your mom call you?"
>
> "Nothing. She didn't like me and called me ugly names."
>
> "Like what?"
>
> "Slut, spoiled brat, and such." The tears started to well up in Lola's eyes.
>
> Lola's father suddenly disappeared and never came back home. Lola's mother was angry and blamed the father's abandonment on everyone else, particularly Lola, and did not take responsibility for anything that had happened in the relationship. Lola at 27 had been through four marriages and had three children and no support system. She looked up with obvious discomfort, and commented, "Perhaps my mother was right—I am a slut."

Children learn and become what they are told unless they can learn, with help, to sort out information, emotions, and feelings, work through the maze of hurts and pain, and move toward creating their own lives.

Family members are connected to each other through a network of smaller subsystems: the husband–wife subsystem, the parent–child subsystems, the sibling subsystems, the grandparent–grandchild subsystems, and so forth. Together they constitute a family system, with the individuals and subsystems functioning as interdependent parts. A change in one part of the system is likely to have an effect on other parts of the system and bring about significant changes in the entire family unit.

> Thirty-eight-year-old Sally desperately wanted to get married and have children. She was afraid that her biological clock was running down, but she seemed incapable of developing a long-term relationship with a man. In therapy she mentioned that her father had been unemployed off and on throughout her childhood. He had seasonal jobs in summer and would be unemployed in the winter months. The money would run low and her mother would nag her father and call him names. The mother's meager income could not really make ends meet. Her father would promise to get a job during the winter months, but most often he would lie in front of the TV, eating chips and drinking beer. Sally's mother constantly said that "men are useless and I have no use for them." Eventually, the couple divorced and the mother struggled with two jobs to provide for four children. Sally added that both her brothers were continually unemployed, but her younger sister was doing well. Sally's fear of a relationship with a man stemmed from her childhood myths of "men being—useless," which affected her life choices and decisions. In many ways the attitudes and behaviors of the family

system affected all the members of the family as they grew up and made their way in the world.

A family system is a dynamic group of people who, with their intellectual, emotional, and behavioral processes, mutually interact. The family system itself has a basic need to adapt, survive, and maintain itself; thus it takes action and behaves as if it were an entity. When conflict arises between the needs of the different family members and the goals the family has for itself, the family system may attempt to regulate and control the behavior of those members who seem to be obstructing the goals. Control of the family is maintained by its rules and regulations, by its communication patterns, and by feedback. For example, if Johnny asks about his alcoholic uncle, the response may be that the uncle "just drinks a little," accompanied by a stern look that tells Johnny he cannot talk about it anymore. All families have goals that govern their existence. Some are explicit and constantly reiterated; others may be unspoken or even unconscious, but there is always an agenda that regulates behavior. For example, "We want to have a perfect family"; "We want our children to excel"; "Children should be seen and not heard"; "Children are the property of their parents and therefore should be obedient under all circumstances"; "There are problems in the family but they are secrets."

Attitudes toward self and others begin at home. If a child's self-esteem is undermined, he or she begins to believe the worst as he or she grows older. Children often have a dependency on their parents, and believe their parents are there to protect and provide for them.

The case of a multimillionaire will help us understand how being a part of the family system can have a tremendous impact on how we relate to others and how we create our relationships with others.

> Harry grew up in a family that taught him that money was very important, and that every penny should be saved for a rainy day. His parents divorced, and his mother remarried, but Harry lived with his father. Although Harry was well educated and became a professional, he had a problem with spending money. If he could walk and save gas money he would. If he had to, he would park twenty blocks away and walk to a meeting even if he felt ill, because he always remembered: "Save your money for a rainy day, because people are like vultures and they can eat you up." Another message he heard from his father was that women were spendthrifts. "Money can dry up quickly. Be suspicious of every woman you meet." Harry internalized these viewpoints and lived his life accordingly. At 45, he was divorced like his father. "I've had nothing but bad luck with women. I've never been able to trust them. My second wife, like my first, divorced me because I kept accusing her of extravagance. It was stupid of me but that's the way I was. She would go out and buy a purse or some expensive cosmetics, and I started thinking and then talking about bankruptcy court."

We learn various ways of being from our parents and caretakers. When giving and taking is skewed in our relationships at home, the result is pain. When we create significant relationships, we carry in our minds all that we learned about relationships. Lacking the capability to understand the background of their family of origin—

particularly if it is dysfunctional—children may carry on the patterns in the families they subsequently create.

Pain and strife in families affect children's sense of self. Adult children from such families often carry the stigma and legacy of toxic relationships.

Sexuality and intimacy are intermeshed within the lifestyle of family members. All people have an innate sexual drive, but our sexual attitudes are largely shaped by our family of origin. When adult family members are intimate, they can share feelings with each other without fear of being ridiculed, and feel respected and loved for who they are. By observation and participation, children learn about love, happiness, deceit, and pain as well as sexual attitudes in a family.

> Erin was puzzled and filled with fear, much like a child who needed reassurance. She asked herself again and again, "Where did I fail? What did I do wrong?" followed by a torrent of tears. This was Erin's second marriage and it appeared she had married "the wrong man" again. David, her second husband, had run out on her, taking with him all her savings and the few luxury items they had managed to buy. He apparently fell in love with a young woman from the gym where he worked out. Although unemployed, it did not affect him too much as his wife earned a large salary, but intimacy and sex had long disappeared from the marriage, replaced by anger and resentment on both sides. Her ridicule of his inability to find a job made him feel less of a man. He sought reassurance, and found it in the form of a pretty 19-year-old, Sandy, who was flattered to listen to the problems of an older man. Soon David was dressing up for Sandy and finally decided to leave his wife. A note on their bed

informed Erin that he was tired of her and was leaving for good. No apologies, no explanation, just a curt note to say good-bye. Andrea, his teenage stepdaughter, was overlooked as if she did not exist. In fact, she was left behind to pick up the pieces of her mother's fragmented ego.

As her mother continued to cry, Andrea thought, petrified in her own fear, "Are all men like this?" She racked her brains trying to visualize her own father, who had disappeared from her life a few years before, leaving his wife and daughter without financial resources. He called Andrea sporadically after he left, but after a few months even this contact stopped. What is Andrea's view of marriage, men, and children? What choices would Andrea make when she was ready to go out on her own?

Life is complex. We all live through different types of family situations that have an effect on how we view people, life, and ourselves. We are, in short, part of a family system—with its rules, regulations, relationships, and feelings—that forms a unique tapestry for each of us. Sexuality is an integral part of this tapestry, and enters all human relationships, not just the most intimate. It is fundamental in the family and a principal root of self-esteem and identity. Sexual interaction is obviously basic for the perpetuation of the family and society itself, but rules and regulations are required for the good of the individual and the community.

SEX AND THE LIFE CYCLE

Attitudes toward sexuality begin within one's own family of origin. Attitudes and behaviors that children view between parents and other adults become for them models of intimacy and sexuality. Sexuality is a natural expression of humanity. It can be approached with pleasure and good sense or with limitlessly distorted emotions and damaging attitudes. When attitudes, whether constructive or destructive, are shared by a large group of people they become part of that group's culture.

This can include complex and obscure ways of viewing and developing sexuality. Every aspect of human development is dependent, to a degree, on what went before it, and this adds to the uniqueness of experiences of different individuals. When Anne saw her father going into the bathroom to use the toilet while she was in the shower, she felt uneasy. Her uneasiness turned to fear when he began to pull open the shower curtains to look at her nude body. At 10 years of age she began to feel ashamed of her body and her growing sexuality. As an adult she was never comfortable with her body or with anyone with whom she shared intimate sexual moments.

To comprehend how each person becomes a sexual being, certain fundamental principles must be understood. Sexuality is intertwined with emotions. Thus psychosexual development happens through interactions between internal and external forces; this in turn leads to the formation of sexual attitudes and behavior throughout life.

The Newborn Infant. Development of an infant's rudimentary ego takes place as a result of both innate and external variables, and there is an innate but somewhat variable timetable through which complex ego capacities unfold. These include thought, perception, the capacity to distinguish fantasy from reality, and a number of functions relating to coping and adaptation of self to the environment. Ego development in an infant is heavily dependent upon the learning experiences to which the child is exposed. The ability of infants to cope effectively with themselves and others is shaped by their interaction with their parents, caretakers, and other significant people. The effects of a healthy ego or a faulty ego are seen at every point in a person's life, in a broad sweep of sexual adaptations and maladaptations. Healthy sexual adaptations take place when children's growth and sexual development are enhanced with nurturing, concern, and warmth.

Maladjustments, however, whether emotional or sexual, have their basis in a number of factors. Pain, fear, anger, or guilt become easily associated with disturbances in a person's psyche and this can lead to and lay the groundwork for disturbed development. None of the developmental changes takes place in isolation. Anything of significance to a human being ultimately proceeds from and involves his or her relationships with others. The child learns quickly what is acceptable and what is not. Children know what will be rewarded and what will not. In a dramatic, horrifying situation, a neurotic mother with a puritan, abusive upbringing scalded the fingers of her infant child in hot water because the 3-month-old touched his penis repeatedly. According to the mother, "Young children should learn very young . . . what will be disapproved of and punished." The results of developmental influences are never static and they lead to specific structures and limitations that constantly renew themselves in interactions with others. Any self-defeating behavior reflects an early beginning, and achieves a new and current reality each time it occurs, producing the predictable result that in turn reinforces it. Some of these interactions between parents and infants influence the child's emerging sexuality.

The knowledge that a new baby is male or female sets into motion in each parent a complex and never-ending series of responses made up of unconscious preconceptions and expectations that become associated with the child's being a girl or a boy. A child's developing sexual identity is a very complex structure that is formed of both conscious and unconscious components.

The most fundamental form of core gender identity is the deep and unalterable sense of being male or female. As a child begins to identify with his or her biological sex, certain behaviors and attitudes will be categorized as appropriate and others as inappropriate. A portion of this sex-role behavior is an expression of innate differences, but the bulk of the behavior is learned through parental and cultural pressures and observations.

As Masters and colleagues (1988) indicate, "Every person has sexual feelings, attitudes, and beliefs, but everyone's experience of sexuality is unique because it is processed through an intensely personal perspective. This perspective comes from both private, personal experience and public social resources. It is impossible to understand human sexuality without recognizing its multidimensional nature" (p. 3).

Sexuality in infancy is closely tied to sensuous closeness of parent and child through holding, clinging, and cuddling. Parent–child bonding begins at birth and extends to include nursing, bathing, dressing, and other physical interactions between parent and newborn child. As Masters and colleagues (1988) indicate, very young children respond quite naturally to a variety of sources of physical sensation with signs of sexual arousal. For example, it is common for baby boys to have erections while they are nursing. This may be alarming to some parents, but the fact is that the sensation of cuddling close to the warmth and softness of the mother's body and the intense neurological stimulation of sucking (the lips are well endowed with sensory nerve endings) combine to send out messages to the brain that are pleasurable and that activate sexual reflexes. In female infants there is clitoral erection and vaginal lubrication that also occurs during nursing, which indicates that this pattern is not restricted to one gender. Similar reflex sexual activation may occur when babies are bathed, powdered, diapered, or playfully bounced around (Masters et al. 1988). As Martinson (1981) points out, "The infant is too young to be consciously aware of the encounter, and therefore no socio-erotic awakening can be said to occur" (p. 26). However, what is important is how parents respond when they observe these sexual reflexes during infancy. These parental responses become a part of the child's earliest sexual learning. When a parent is shocked or disapproving, the baby is apt to react in a manner that conveys discomfort. When parents react calmly, they help the child feel accepted.

The various ways in which parents and relatives relate to children are culturally determined.

> Betty, who was severely punished from babyhood for touching herself, found herself, at age 30, unable to create a relationship with a man and was always overcome with shame and guilt when she was sexually aroused. She masked her shame and guilt with a coldness and stiffness that turned men away, although she was an attractive woman.

It is impossible to overestimate the importance of this early groundwork that provides a healthy or unhealthy basis for future attitudes toward one's own body and the bodies of others and also toward what might be hoped for in a physical relationship. When children develop physical contacts with the mother that are inadequate or rejecting, the children may develop a permanent inability to trust closeness with anyone for fear of disappointment. This mistrust may also express itself in wary, hostile avoidance of love involvements. There could be a desperate, dependent clinging to any possible love object, or an unfulfilled search for the close relationship that never existed with the mother.

Early Childhood. By the time children are 4 years old, they have magical notions of how babies are born. They often believe that the stork brings the baby. They also participate in genital play, which begins as a solitary activity and then appears later in games such as "Show me yours and I'll show you mine" and "Doctor." Masters and colleagues (1988) indicate that conversations with 3- and 4-year-olds reveal that children are well aware of the sensual feelings brought about by genital stimulation. However, they are also aware of parental disapproval of genital play and may be confused by parents who tell them to be aware of their bodies but exclude the genitals from such awareness. While it is important for parents to educate children about socially appropriate behaviors in public, a severe and negative attitude toward sex makes children view their genitals as being "dirty." Telling a child, "Wash your hands after you go," although hygienic, may also create the situation where children begin to view their genital organs as dirty.

When children begin to go to nursery school or daycare centers, they are apt to confront many situations that, from an adult's perspective, have sexual overtones. For example, Jack sneaks behind a girl and pulls up her dress to see her underpants and does this with a great deal of giggling. In all likelihood, Jack is either being curious or testing the adult caretaker.

> A mother lost her temper with her own son, Neal, when he pulled up his younger sister's dress to look at her panties. Neal was 3½ years old but the mother took him for a psychiatric exam, insisting he was "abnormal." She was angry with him for years and called him "oversexed." Neal, uncomfortable with this title, kept away from girls. Why did Neal's mother do this? Because Neal reminded his mother of her ex-husband, and all the negative feelings she felt toward him she expressed toward Neal—the new target of her hatred.

As children enter the school years, they tend to incorporate cultural norms concerning modesty, and seem less interested in relations with the opposite sex. At 5 or 6 they also develop ideas about sex based upon what they observe between their parents or between parent and partner and others. Children learn a healthy way of viewing emotional and physical intimacy if they observe their parents hugging, kissing, and being loving toward each other; but if parents are always quarreling with each other and children hear statements like "Don't touch me," it has a negative effect.

Sex and the School-age Child. By the time children are 6 or 7 years old they have acquired an understanding of the basic anatomic differences between the sexes and show a strong sense of modesty about body exposure. Again, parental attitudes and practices regarding nudity in the home influence the child's self-consciousness. A number of children, however, participate in sexual experimentation, finding out whatever they can about sexuality. "Childhood sex play is not psychologically harmful under ordinary circumstances and is probably a valuable psychosocial experience in developmental terms. However, psychological harm can come from harsh parental reaction" (Masters et al. 1988, p. 129). Parental reactions to the discovery of sex play in schoolchildren usually operate on a double standard. Girls are often strongly cautioned against sexual play, while boys tend to get mixed messages from their parents. They may be warned and even punished for such behaviors, or, with a hint of resignation or pride, parents might say, "Boys will be boys." The unspoken approval given to boys to experiment sexually has rarely been directed to school-age girls. Money (1980) indicates that the years before puberty (preadolescence), which can vary from 10 to 12 or 13, is a time of sexual prudery, where sexual curiosity and sex play go underground.

Adolescent Sexuality. The period of quiescence is followed by adolescent sexuality, a period of discovery and awakening in which intellectual and emotional maturation are combined with physical development and maturation. The essential aspect of adolescence is that it is visible in the sexual sphere.

While earlier experiences of sexuality were primarily self-focused, interest in potential partners becomes evident during adolescence. In a continuation from childhood, the majority of adolescents masturbate to frequent sexual dreams and fantasies (Wiederman 1995). These mental rehearsals are probably important developmental steps in the adolescent's start toward relating sexually to others. During adolescence the first sexual interactions are likely to occur as the individual begins developing a repertoire of sexual behaviors (DeLamater and MacCorquodale 1979).

Adolescents move through a phase of establishing a personal identity. They struggle for independence from their parents, and look to peer groups for support and guidance. They are enthusiastic about correcting the mistakes of the older generations and like all other generations before them, they set up their own rules, expectations, and social controls. Adolescents usually have a need to be liked by their friends, and their desire for freedom can be curbed by other adolescents in their group. Peer pressure varies from one area to another, from one ethnic group to another, and from one socioeconomic and religious group to another. In some groups the code of sexual conduct is traditional, with a high premium on female virginity, and almost all sexual activity is limited to "meaningful" relationships. If this code is not followed by girls, they develop a reputation that says that they are an "easy lay," and are misused by boys. However, another group may consider sex a status symbol, the "uninitiated" versus those who are "in the know." Whenever a teenager is ready for sex, it reflects personal values, moral reasoning, and fear of negative consequences and also the fear of involvement in a romantic attachment. Those who become sexually active at a young age often appear to place a high premium on personal independence (Reinisch 1990).

In adolescence, according to *The Kinsey Report on Sex* (Reinisch 1990) about 82 percent of boys have participated in masturbation, while only 20 percent of the girls have done so. Petting, which is described as erotic arousal without sexual intercourse, is a common form of physical contact between females and males.

It is important to keep in mind that adolescence varies enormously from culture to culture, and from one historical period to another. In some cultures there is no adolescence as we know it; people move from childhood to adult status after a brief rite of passage. At the other extreme is contemporary American society, in which the transition from childhood to adulthood lasts for many years. At the same time, teenagers are having sex—and babies—more frequently than ever before. These are some of the major sub-variations of our culture.

Sexual intercourse can be a time of happiness, pleasure, intimacy, and satisfaction, or it can be a source of worry, discomfort, disappointment, and a great deal of guilt.

> Tina, a young woman of 17, fell in love with a young man and, after some heavy drinking, petting, and intercourse, became pregnant. Coming from a conservative Baptist background, she was shocked and panicked. Repressing the memory of the actual sexual encounter, she had a quick abortion. Even though she fell in love again, she could not have sex or physical closeness or warmth as she froze again and again thinking of her abortion—her secret. That secret was toxic; she could not discuss it with her family or friends, but it consumed her and took over her life completely. Although her parents noticed her avoidance of male relationships, no one questioned her because discussion of sexuality or topics surrounding it was taboo in the family.

Early and Middle Adulthood. Early adulthood is a critical time in a person's life, in which important choices need to be made, including marriage, occupation, and lifestyle. The early years of adulthood are for some a time of sexual uncertainty, but of sexual satisfaction for others. Often this is the period when conflict over attitudes of sexual guilt or immorality, carried over from earlier years, is expressed.

Many people in this age group do get married, and attitudes they draw from in their own homes are those they have observed and developed through their own experiences. During this stage people also cohabit, and this includes casual or temporary involvement, and preparation or substitution for marriage. According to Weiderman (1995), more than 90 percent of Americans marry at least once; dating and cohabitation are commonly a means of securing a spouse. The sexual activities and frequency of sexual behaviors vary both among individuals and during phases of adulthood as people's priorities and relationship status change. Though large majority of Americans marry at some point, at any given time a significant portion of the population is single (Martin and Bumpass 1989), and the sexual experiences of married, divorced, and never-married persons sometimes vary widely (Smith 1991).

Around 40 years of age people enter a period of transition; either couples are happy with each other or they are looking for someone else. This is a particularly difficult period for men, who go through an appraisal of goals, accomplishments, and experiences. This is called the midlife crisis, and some men, afraid of becoming old, turn to younger women for love and sexual satisfaction, believing their wives are at fault and a younger partner can help heat up the passion. Also, in our culture, younger women married to older men is not frowned upon, although older women marrying younger men usually is.

Also overlooked during this period is the severe sexual burnout in some couples, often accompanied by depression. They lose interest in all sexual activities and may suffer from loss of appetite and loss of sleep.

> Dillon had been a successful businessman. He was married and had four children. He loved his wife, Marcie, and spent a great deal of time with her. They had an active sexual life for seventeen years but in the last three years matters began to change. Dillon

> was overcome with business problems and did not participate in any sexual activity for two full years. He became depressed when his wife began to question him. The financial problems of his business seemed to overwhelm him and he began to lose his appetite and sleep poorly. In therapy he said that he was burned out, emotionally and sexually.

During this period men and women who have been content with being single may become ready to make serious commitments as they see life as running out on them.

> Forty-three-year-old Janice decided to marry her professor, Sam, who was in his early sixties. They faced a number of problems stemming from their different cultural backgrounds: she was Hungarian and he was American. She talked about wanting to have a baby before "my time runs out," whereas Sam, who was widowed and had two adult children, was not willing to go through the parenting role again. In therapy, Janice lamented that her parents let her marry this "old man" because they wanted to see her "settled." With much discussion and compromise, Janice finally became pregnant. Although Sam was initially very skeptical, his wife's pregnancy brought for him and her a new buoyancy in life.

In midlife, women and men go through some physical changes. Although there is much disagreement about the effects of menopause on sexuality, recent research does not support the notion that sexual interest declines during this period in a woman's life; for some women there is an increase in sexual desires (Cutler et al. 1987).

In men the normal patterns of reproductive functioning are quite different. About 5 percent of men over the age of 60 experience a condition called male climacteric, which resembles female menopause. This can be followed by poor appetite, loss of potency, and reduction in sexual desire.

Later Adulthood. Just as we know very little about childhood sexuality because of cultural taboos, so sexuality in old age has not been extensively explored by researchers. Although there is cultural negativism about sex and romance among older couples, there is also a measure of exciting sex for the elderly. The extent to which individuals remain sexually active in their senior years appears to depend on a combination of factors, such as personal preference, health status, availability of a partner, living arrangements, and cultural expectations (Winn and Newton 1982). Although the act of sexual intercourse may take a slightly longer time, intimacy, making love, holding, hugging, and embracing all become part of the person's sexual and intimacy patterns (Winn and Newton 1982).

Sex is more than an act in which a person experiences pleasure; it becomes the basis for love, intimacy, and the ability to procreate. When people fall in love, they usually care about each other and are willing to live a lifetime with their partners. However, a large number of people do not know how to work at a relationship and keep it alive and healthy. When faced with problems, some couples who have experienced few conflicts in their family of origin, or have not learned how to fight fairly, are willing to give up. When they make a commitment for permanency, this becomes a limited and convenient way to suit each other's needs. Intimacy means that we can be who we are in a relationship and allow the other person to do the same. As Lerner (1989) mentions, "An intimate relationship is one in which neither party silences, sacrifices, or betrays the self and each party expresses strength and vulnerability in a balanced way" (p. 19).

STRESS AND INTERACTIONAL PATTERNS

People do not go to school to learn what is involved in marriage and parenthood. Also, people have different notions of what a marriage means. At the least, marriage can be viewed in three different ways: one view of marriage is that it is a divine institution and marriage is sacred; second, marriage has a social meaning and is viewed in terms of family and community; and third, there is an individual meaning, with demands made on the marriage subordinated to the well-being and happiness of the individuals. When couples make a commitment to each other, they are assuming that the other person has similar notions of commitment. Quite often, this is not even discussed. Sooner or later, every relationship gets tested, and there are different types of stressors that couples can face.

What is stress? According to Hans Selye (1991), "My definition of *stress* is the *nonspecific* (that is, common) *result of any demand upon the body*, be the effect mental or somatic" (p. 22). It is important to bear in mind that there are a number of dissimilar situations that contribute to stress. Emotional arousal, effort, fatigue, pain, fear, concentration, humiliation, loss of blood, and even great or unexpected success are capable of producing stress. No single factor can, in itself, be pinpointed as the cause or reaction as such.

When most individuals speak of being under stress they are usually referring to external demands that impinge on them, including pressure at work, sudden unemployment, or illness of a family member. The study of stress coincides with the popular view and focuses on triggers that provoke emotional, behavioral, and physiological reactions (Roskies 1991).

The Institute of Medicine report *Stress and Human Health* (Elliott and Eisdorfer 1982) classifies stressors according to duration: (1) acute, time-limited stressors, such as a job interview or a visit to a doctor for a medical check-up; (2) stress sequences or a series of events that occur over an extended period of time as a result of an initiating stress trigger, including multiple factors such as residential, financial, job, parental, and social changes that can follow a divorce; (3) chronic intermittent stressors, such as periodic arguments with a spouse or a weekly budget meeting; and (4) chronic stressors, such as permanent disabilities and marital strife, which may or may not be initiated by a discrete event and which persist continuously over a long time. Long-lasting stressors can have more serious consequences than acute, time-limited ones. Stress also depends upon quality rather than on duration alone, and the quantity of stresses, that is, the accumulation of stressors, requires more adjustment eventually than the quality or duration. When a person faces a number and diversity of stressors, it can perhaps make him or her self-defeating or stronger.

> Donald and Minnie had been married for a short time when they realized that their dreams of buying a beautiful home and having children had to be postponed as Donald was laid off from work. Minnie was surprised and disappointed. She had married a professional and felt that he was not "worthy" to hold on to a job. She was a teacher and could not comprehend how he could lose his job after three months of marriage. At first she tried to be under-

standing, but became less so when he demanded that they move out of the area so he could find a better job elsewhere. Minnie did not wish to move; she had family and friends living in the same area. They quarreled about it and he accused her of being more loyal to her family and her friends than to him. In return she called him "lazy" and "unworthy" for losing his job. Before they realized it, the quarrel ballooned into an ugly situation in which they were calling each other names.

Donald felt unworthy and attempted to keep the house looking clean, but Minnie was overwhelmed with money problems and continued to harp on his job situation and lack of effort to find a job. Donald, also overwhelmed and angry, started to draw out their savings secretly and began to use the money for drinking.

When people are under stress they become very vulnerable. These stressors make people more needy, and ensure heightening of the expectations they brought to the relationship. Being unemployed is a situational stressor and can cause a great deal of conflict. It also requires making adjustments, acknowledging the problems and stresses each one feels, and planning for an emergency. Other situational stressors can include an unplanned pregnancy, a blizzard, a disagreeable and unpleasant colleague in the workplace, and chronic alcoholism in a family member.

Other kinds of stressful situations include migration, job change, physical distance from an extended family, and prolonged illness in a family member. Each takes a toll on the family and, in different ways, on each family member. Quite often, people respond to stressors in ways they have learned and acquired in their family of origin. This can include defensiveness, anger, and inability to forgive others. Unless couples and family members learn to develop their own fair strategies of working with conflicts, their intimate family life will eventually be affected. There are also stresses in the transition from being single to being married, or from living together to being married.

In families in which children are viewed as possessions, it is convenient for parents to take out their stress on their children, as one angry young woman told me in therapy.

> Mollie was the youngest of twelve children, but somehow, even as a child, she felt that her father did not like her, for he always picked on her and took out his anger on her. She told me, sobbing loudly at her traumatic recollections, how her father had abused her. If he had a bad day in the office, she could sense his stress as he drove the car into the garage. The tires would screech as he brought the car to a stop and he would slam the door loudly. Mollie would run and hide herself because she was afraid of being beaten. There had been too many previous experiences of being the victim of his temper. How did this happen? The mother would get anxious and blame the children for anything the father found annoying, like the TV set being on. His wife would fumble and pick on her youngest daughter, saying perhaps Mollie had turned the TV on, or whatever he was complaining about. Immediately he would pounce on his daughter, beating her for her "mistake." Her mother would feebly protest against this behavior but would never try to stop him. At 27, Mollie did not question why her mother

picked on her to be the victim of the father's temper, but only saw her father as cruel.

As such incidents increased, Mollie learned to hide herself when she heard the car tires screech. One day she remembered hiding in the closet, hoping her father would go away. He was complaining about the people in his office, particularly his boss, and then suddenly switched tones as he irritably said that his daughter was hiding from him. He called out to Mollie and she continued to hide, hardly breathing, in the dark closet. Suddenly she felt her father's harsh hand pull her out, and he was breathing heavily when he told her that she should know better than hide herself. With that comment he started to beat her and she began to urinate with fear. This made him angrier, and his beatings became more severe as he told her to stop urinating, but she had no control. Afterwards he made her clean up the carpet but would not let her change her jeans and punished her by sending her to school in her soiled pants.

Mollie hated him and everything he represented. He always told his daughters he would kill them if they came home pregnant. He wanted all of them to be virgins until they married. Mollie's face distorted with pain and she cried that she hated her father and all the pain he had caused her. Her only way to exact revenge was to show him she would live her life the way she wanted. By her fourteenth birthday she was no longer a virgin. Her father died soon after that of a heart attack, and Mollie looked at me with hatred in her eyes and said it was the best day of her life. She did not cry but wanted to celebrate the passing away of an evil man.

How did this affect Mollie? She used men for sex

as much as they used her. At 27, she had been to bed with over a hundred men and was afraid that she might die of AIDS. Ironically, though her mother had been a passive partner in Mollie's abuse, Mollie saw her mother as helpless and was willing to take care of her.

To my question, "Didn't your mother tell your father you were not responsible for anything chaotic that upset him?" Mollie said that her mother was trying to protect herself from her husband's anger and was therefore blameless. "My mother was a better parent than my father ever was." With that statement she sealed her loyalty packet with her mother. Her parents did not have a good marriage, she said, they did not make love even once after she was born. "How do you know?" I asked. "My mother always spoke about it to me and my sisters! We all knew he was a bad man. He had a mistress. Most men are like my father. I will not marry because no man can really be faithful." Mollie ended the session with all the myths she had learned about men while growing up.

Myths are fairly integrated beliefs that people hold in families regarding their role and status, and are commonly unchallenged. Thus, in different ways, a family myth represents the manner in which a family appears to its members and is a part of the inner image of the group, that is, an image that all family members contribute to and attempt to preserve. A family myth refers to identified roles that family members take on, individually or collectively, consciously or subconsciously, for the sake of the family (Pillari 1986). Thus, in Mollie's case, the mother was seen as the deprived one and Mollie was comfortable looking out for her. Her loyalty to her mother was strong and unfailing. To be loyal to her mother she had to be single, because her mother constantly lamented that all men were bad.

INVISIBLE LOYALTIES AND INTERGENERATIONAL PATTERNS

One of the major concepts of familial dynamics is *family loyalty,* introduced into the therapeutic literature by Boszormenyi-Nagy and Krasner (1986). Loyalty as viewed by them is synonymous with the essential irrefutability of family ties. However easily a person displaces or transfers his filial loyalties to therapist, boss, nor partner, the primary commitment of family loyalty remains untouched.

Loyalty, as Boszormenyi-Nagy and Krasner describe it, is not based on a sense of loyalty as explained by the psychology of attachment or attraction, nor is it based on the inspired dependence or submission of the weaker person as in feudal loyalty to king or high nobility. Loyalty, in a sense, can be described as preferential commitment to a relationship that is based on *indebtedness* born out of *earned merit.* Parents give birth to children and become obligated to their survival and nurturance. Parents, in turn, earn their child's commitment in return for the mother's or father's unique, unrepayable contribution. In addition to this, family members carry with them invisible loyalties developed in their family of origin. Intimacy and family loyalty are interconnected when a family member continues to be loyal to his or her family of origin. For example, if the first and most important relationship taught children is that the people they love will hurt them and be terrifyingly unpredictable, that experience might affect them permanently. A large number of children of alcoholics, for example, are afraid of becoming close to another person. All successful adult relationships between partners, as well as among family members, require a significant degree of vulnerability, trust, and openness, and these are the very elements that an alcoholic household destroys.

> Seven-year-old Tendra was terrified of her father, Stuart, who was an alcoholic. She saw how he abused her mother and her older brother. Her mother would talk about how painful life was for her because of Stuart, but she was too afraid not to give him money for liquor. If she did not, he would ransack the house looking for money, and would sell things in the house to fulfill his alcoholic needs. Tendra grew up in mortal fear and hatred of her father. On his birthday she drew a picture of him and in her childish hand wrote, "Happy birthday you UGLY monster" and showed it to her 10-year-old brother, who laughed hysterically because he did not like his father either. Their father, in a half-drunken stupor, hearing them laugh, came to check on them and found the picture. His daughter's drawing infuriated him, and he beat her black-and-blue. He also made her eat the paper so that she would never do anything like that again.
>
> Stuart did not forget this for a long time, and would fly into a fury whenever he saw his daughter. Tendra learned to hide from her father and often sat in the bathroom with the door closed; months passed and the father began to forget the incident, but Tendra, of course, never forgot. As a result, when Tendra became an adult she was afraid of creating relationships, particularly with men. However, she met a man, Jim, a recovering alcoholic, in a hospital where she worked as a nurse. Shortly thereafter she

married him. He was emotionally unavailable but the two of them created the illusion of a relationship without confronting his or her terror of true intimacy.

Although Jim claimed that he had "recovered" from alcoholism, Tendra quickly found out that her husband closely resembled her father—often terrifying, and wonderful at times. By picking a volatile and abusive man Tendra was repeating the familiar patterns of her childhood and guaranteeing that she would never have to risk entering the uncharted journey of true intimacy. Her loyalty to her family of origin was very much intact and affected every aspect of her life.

As I have indicated (Pillari 1994), in some families there are also a few "secret" emotional themes. Unpleasant topics are never discussed. Families talk about keeping themselves "worry-free," and have many fears about discussing taboo topics. These may be the result of longstanding multigenerational conflicts, or may relate to current problems. In such families a loyal family member internalizes its spirit and expectations. This person also develops a set of specific attitudes and behaviors to comply with the internalized injunctions. Failure to comply with the family obligations leads to guilt feelings and enormous pressures to conform. Thus in families there are layers of loyalty. Loyalty commitments are invisible but are held together by strong threads that blend complex pieces of relationship behavior. To understand the functions of a group of people, we need to know how they are bound together and what loyalty means to them. Every person maintains an account of what has been invested in his or her system and what has been withdrawn in the form of support received or exploitative use of others. This may be classified as invisible accounts of obligations and affects intimate relationships.

In some families the fundamental loyalty commitment is to the maintenance of the group itself. Boszormenyi-Nagy and Krasner (1986) indicate that people must go beyond conscious behavioral manifestations and specific issues if they want to understand the meaning of basic loyalty commitments. What may appear to an outsider as shocking and destructive behavior toward a family member may not be experienced as such by those involved if it conforms to a basic family loyalty pattern.

> Fifty-year-old Kevin was disinherited by his parents, although he was the oldest child and an only son who had run the family business for a number of years. Kevin provided for his parents and his married sister and her family, although she had an able-bodied husband whom the family accepted as "good-looking but lazy." When Kevin learned of the secret disinheritance from his family when his father died, everyone, including his mother—who played a key role in the disinheritance—claimed not to be aware of the will, although a similar will, disinheriting her son, had been drawn by her on the same day. When her disinherited son left in anger, disbelief, and pain, the mother claimed that he had "just gone for a short time" and they were a very happy family. Family myths are generally accompanied by a taboo against investigating or challenging the validity of the beliefs. If anyone challenges the myth, like Kevin, he is seen as disloyal or disturbed, and the family waits patiently until he comes back to his senses.

In another case, Susan felt that her obligation to be the family peacemaker robbed her of her chance to meet her own needs. Peacemaking was a function assigned to her in early childhood. She heard constant comments as a child that she was good at settling problems and making peace among her siblings and later between her parents. As she grew older she continued to perform this role in most relationships, to her detriment. In her relationships with men she gave in easily for the sake of peace and reduction of conflict; however, it led to conflict avoidance in her life, and her ability to be assertive was thwarted, which in turn affected her ability to be intimate with anyone. Although it re-created a sense of resentment in her as her family and friends took her for granted, Susan was still invisibly loyal to her own family of origin, which led to poor relationships for her and also obstructed her road to individuation.

When many taboos and secrets rule a household, the family members are likely to be dysfunctional to some degree and to suffer from low self-esteem. Such people have not differentiated themselves as individuals in the family. They may solidify a relationship in which the boundaries between self and others become blurred and the uniqueness of a person is acknowledged only covertly, if at all. In such families there is an expectation of family loyalty even if it smothers the family members.

Through observation, experiencing, and being a part of a family system, children also learn from parents ways of giving and taking. Often there is one-sided giving, nurturing, and devotion that earn a parent's credit. As parents age, however, children are faced with obligations for that one-sided consideration. Like the child they reared, the aging parents may be limited in their capacity and have expectations that their child(ren) may take care of them; at times such expectations may be unrealistic. This issue is made more complex by conflicts of interest for the adult child who wants to offer his sick or aging parent care. As one woman said, "My husband and I spent our lives doing for our children, our church, and our families." She was in her early sixties and added, "Now we want to live a little, travel, and have some fun. But my parents are in their late eighties and continue to make me feel guilty. I am their only child. What do I owe me? What do I owe them?" (Boszormenyi-Nagy and Krasner 1986, p. 87).

As Boszormenyi-Nagy and Spark specified in their book *Invisible Loyalties* (1984), people feel obligated to carry out their duties toward their parents. Even when there has been pain, sham, and shame, the loyalties continue to be strong, although they may be invisible. A 30-year-old woman who had been in an incestuous relationship with her father for most of her childhood and teenage years went back to see him when he was on his deathbed. She commented, "I was angry with him for a long time, but at least he loved me and gave me things. All I know about my mother is that she was never there for me and was always very distant. I guess I will take care of him in spite of the fact he was sexually abusive to me. . . . I have forgiven him, and it's time for me to go visit him and spend time with him before he dies."

Human beings are very complex in their loyalties and behaviors. To weave through intimacy issues in relationships requires a great deal of effort, patience, and the ability to think through, understand, and work through family backgrounds and patterns.

CHAPTER TWO

Sexual and Intimacy Problems in Couples

I love you but the awful silence falls not when I am alone but when I am with you

—*Sheldon, 1982*

JON WAS MARRIED BUT unemployed and apparently very unhappy. One day, in agony, he confessed to his wife that he had been to a bar and solicited a prostitute. Explaining to his horrified wife that he went there only because he did not like himself and "felt like a housewife," but sitting in the bar and staring at the "low-down" people there, he felt better about himself. What should Nina do? Divorce him? Undergo therapy with him, or send a detective behind his back to follow him? How did such a situation arise? What happened to this couple's ability to communicate with each other in hard times? What is the role of the husband and wife in this situation? They have four children—how could they explain anything to the children? In the first place, what incidents prompted this to happen?

Who is Jon? Jon had faced a number of rejections growing up, and without a job he was nagged by his wife and felt rejected by her and the children. She made him do housework, as he was unemployed. Their communication, which had never been good, failed completely. As a young man Jon had been rejected by his parents as a failure when he did not do well in college. Thus he dropped out and never worked through his issues of rejection, abandonment, and unwantedness. Would he be able to develop an intimate relationship with his wife at all, and how would the couple begin to communicate and rework the marriage? What is the role of trust issues in the family? How does Nina fit in with her husband, and how will she work at the marriage? After the initial shock and anger, and Jon's tearful reassurances that he wanted to be in the marriage, they ended up in couples therapy. In therapy it became clear that neither of them communicated about important matters, like the financial situation in the home. There was no time management, and almost everything was done impulsively. They were a typical "doing" couple. Being involved in activities, they did not find the need for intimate communication. Jon's wife claimed that they discussed all matters in her family while she was growing up, but Jon discouraged any discussion and therefore she stopped trying to raise issues. Halfway through the session she was in tears, complaining how lonely and sad she had felt in the marriage, but she had carried on for the "sake of the children." Jon's unemployment had been an added burden, but Jon was not willing to discuss anything that bothered him and, if given a chance, would lie in bed or watch TV. She repeated that she came from a family where everyone communicated well with each other. Jon looked forlorn and fidgety while his wife spoke. As therapy slowly revealed, Jon came from a family where there was a great deal of strife. Jon's parents were rivals for the children's affection. His parents very subtly set the children against each other and against the other parent. Thus Jon and his mother formed a pair and Jon's sister, Amy, and his father formed another pair. There was constant tension in the family, with undertones of suspicion, anger, and deception. He had even heard that his mother was not satisfied in her sex life with his father. However, on the outside, they presented themselves as a happy family. The distancing, mistrust, anger, and lack of intimacy was a family secret.

Thus communication was limited and intimacy was neglected. Jon felt through his youth that he had to show off to feel loved and had superficial relationships where getting "one up" was the game. These games did not go well with his wife, and long before he lost his job he had shut her out. Their sex life was almost nil, except when it was done mechanically, but their communication of love, caring, nurturing, and intimacy gradually disappeared. Jon and Nina's home life resembled more and more the home that Jon grew up in.

Sexuality begins with our genetic makeup and evolves in unique ways for each of us throughout life, especially as we grow up in families. Good communication and intimacy do not start when a person gets married but rather in their families of origin. Sexuality encompasses many things, including gender; gender identity; sense of self as boy or girl, woman or man; masculinity and femininity as culturally defined; sex roles; sexual preferences; and physical appearances.

"Sex" in the sense of physical pleasure and desire is part of sexuality, but not synonymous with it.

Often adults pretend or behave as if the sexuality that is so closely interrelated to intimacy is not happening. When young children ask innocent questions about sex they are told to "Hush up" or, at times, are punished. Frequently this is only a routine curiosity question for a child. When the young child's question is answered appropriately, the child can begin to view sex as a natural part of life. But when sex is presented as a "forbidden zone," then the area becomes shrouded with mystery, and a child's curiosity often goes underground as he or she begins to get information from outside sources, some healthy and others unhealthy.

As children we learn about sexuality at home in many different ways, based on how adults treat one another. Power struggles begin to be apparent to children, while the parents pretend that children do not understand what is happening in a couple's relationship.

> Alice mentioned in therapy, "I worry about my parents when they go to bed, as I can't sleep."
>
> "Why can't you sleep?"
>
> "Because they fight about sex."
>
> "How do you know?"
>
> "I know because Dad always calls Mom a 'fat chick' and Mom gets angry and she goes downstairs and eats ice cream in the middle of the night. Then Dad will go down and they'll fight some more, and I get scared and I can't sleep."
>
> "What do you think can be done?"
>
> "Dad should listen to Mom and not have sex . . . because Mom says sex is not good."
>
> "How do you know?"

"I heard Mom on the phone when she was talking to Lucy [Mom's friend]."

"If Mom and Dad reassured you that they are working on their issues would that make you comfortable?"

"I don't know . . . but I know Dad should not do sex because it makes Mom sad and angry."

All children are not this fortunate, to get their issues out in the open in therapy and work with them. Often the issues are pushed under the rug, and the child becomes an adult, practicing and developing patterns that he or she watched and consciously or unconsciously learned while growing up.

Sexual interaction is a form of human communication, as is the rest of our behavior. When it is not shrouded in mystery, children, like adults, learn about sex in the normal process of growing up. As a child, my 4-year-old son surprised me when we were driving from New York to Connecticut. We were having a good time singing nursery rhymes. It was almost dusk and we were speeding on the snaky roads in the middle of the woods. Suddenly my son pointed his finger to a spot I had just passed and said, "Mom, stop! Do you see the rabbits? They're mating. You know, making love," and added, "like getting married." I was surprised by his comments and asked how he knew. He looked at me as if I had lost my mind. "Mr. Rogers told us about it on TV." I was amused and surprised but I learned that day that information about sex can be communicated in a manner that helps children accept sex and their own sexuality comfortably and naturally. As my son saw the rabbits and called my attention to their mating, I realized that I could have stifled his innocent communication very easily with the sexual taboos so prevalent in our culture, or with my own anxiety. Fortunately, this did not happen. As he gets older, of course, I expect him to learn when, how, and with whom to discuss sexual matters appropriately.

Thus sexuality and communication are intertwined, an early part of our developmental history. We learn about patterns and ways of talking primarily from the family that surrounds us and from our other social relationships as well as from newspapers, TV, and magazines that enter our homes.

CREATING INTIMACY

There are different ways of creating intimacy with people, including (1) symmetrical intimacy, (2) self-disclosure, and (3) empathy (Goodman and Esterly 1988).

Symmetrical Intimacy. Symmetrical intimacy explains what happens when people first connect. It helps make sense of early mutual attraction or dislike, and brings to light primitive, unwitting, and sometimes embarrassing ways we attach to each other. In many ways symmetrical intimacy is an exciting way of connecting with each other, because the mutual attraction is on an unconscious or preconscious level. Interpersonal symmetry between people is not the same as similarity. It means a balance of needs, a matching of temperaments in people who may be quite different, even opposites, provided that the differences are complementary rather than clashing. For example, Lily and Larry have a good symmetrical relationship. Larry likes to start things and hand them over to his wife, Lily, who takes over the details. She enjoys his dry-witted slow talk and he enjoys her rapid-fire delivery. They like the complementary qualities in each other. Such partners are similar in what they want in the relationship. Couples continuously and automatically check the symmetry between themselves. Sometimes coping with each other helps to provide checks and balances and facilitates their spending a number of years or a lifetime together. In many ways we are still intuitive and animal-like when we first encounter someone who attracts us. Often the prospect of a relationship begins with and is first judged by context, the appearance, and the manner of speech of the other person. Underneath the dating ritual there is generally a preliminary assessment of compatibility. As a new couple engage in general conversation, they are also sizing up each other in terms of their own needs and goals. Sometimes the attraction is based on unmet needs and unresolved issues from one's earlier life experiences. This is also the reason why people who have not thought through their issues in their family of origin gravitate toward a man or woman who resembles their alcoholic father or mother, and don't see it as a problem until they are deeply involved. This is most apparent in couples with intergenerational patterns of alcoholism.

Self-Disclosure. Self-disclosure is a second vital element in the acceleration of intimacy. In self-disclosure there is an attempt to keep matters balanced; however, unilateral disclosure can create a one-way intimacy that is not intimacy at all. Intimacy shrinks when there is a prolonged imbalance in emotional risk-taking. When one person shares life's burdens with another, it can bring them together quickly, but when there is no reciprocation the relationship is no longer balanced. In some cases, when only one person discloses a great deal, the other partner may become overwhelmed or frightened by the disclosure, and the imbalance in communication may destroy the relationship. Intimacy needs symmetry and also reciprocation if it is long-lasting. In intimacy there is also emotional risk-taking, and this may involve carrying the uncomfortable burden of a partner's heavy secrets. It is good to have disclosures that are matched, and accept the burden of disclosure where people wish to carry their share of the load.

Empathy. The third side of intimacy in the Goodman and Esterly scale is empathy. When people make risky disclosures, there must be empathetic understanding. When a person feels understood, then it creates psychological safety and allows vulnerable feelings and minor confessions to come out. The new private information that is shared by risky disclosures allows a greater opportunity to see and confirm similarities, and to make new connections between people. When empathy is not clearly communicated between a couple, there will be trouble in a relationship. When the communication of empathy is reduced, and there is an increase in vulnerability, it can start a chain reaction, leading to a breakdown of the relationship. One type of burden that couples may face occurs when there is a disclosure of past sexual histories.

> When Edwin discussed his past sexual relationships, which had lasted for a minimum of six months, Julia started to confide about her brief and indiscriminate sexual escapades. This upset Edwin, because he was ashamed and confused that the woman he loved was so "loose." He could not appreciate her gift of honesty, and was confused. At times he wanted to discuss it but did not know how. They were completely out of balance. This led to a terrible tilt in the relationship. Julia was scared and felt betrayed by Edwin. On the other hand, he could not empathize with her fear or disclose his

confusion. So they began to get disconnected and distant.

It all started with an imbalance in Edwin's ability to accept the weight of Julia's secrets. If there had been disclosures about an alcohol or gambling problem, this would probably have been better accepted and handled by the couple. But sexual disclosure is a notorious troublemaker that generally impacts on men and women differently. Some couples will not share their sexual past, feeling that "what they don't know won't hurt them. This is a new beginning." There are different points of view on whether this should be discussed at all. Goodman and Esterly (1988) indicate that concealment in long-term relationships is not healthy, but women and men react differently to it. Goodman and Esterly quote Dr. Joyce Brothers, and say that when the man is unfaithful, "after the initial shock, the woman comes to terms with her husband's infidelity. She does not like it, but there it is. It happened. In time, she forgives, although she may never be able to forget. But let a woman be unfaithful and watch her husband's righteous indignation, his angry outrage, his horror" (p. 206).

There is a wide variety and complexity in intimate relations. As Masters and colleagues (1988) indicate, intimacy without romance or sexual interaction is apt to be different from intimacy that accompanies love or romantic love or sexual passion. When two people work or play together and enjoy each other's company, but have little or no exchange of their inner thoughts and feelings, one person may fall in love with the other without expressing that feeling. In a similar fashion, intimacy can be a temporary condition, as when two people sit together on a plane and engage in a very personal conversation, but if they meet later at a cocktail party they may be uncomfortable with their disclosures. However, before people can become intimate, they have to experience intimacy with self.

The ability to form intimate relationships with others depends upon a person's sense of self based on realistic self-knowledge and a reasonable degree of self-acceptance. Such self-awareness helps individuals identify their own needs and feelings and thus enables them to share them with others. Self-acceptance becomes an important building block for interpersonal intimacy, as it allows people to be themselves without pretending to be something other than who and what they are.

People who do not like themselves, or feel ashamed of who they are, have a difficult time establishing and maintaining intimacy because they are preoccupied with trying to prove themselves and trying to gain recognition or respect. Others who do not like themselves may becomes depressed, and may deal with their feelings in ways that block self-awareness. Of course, this does not mean that a person has to be totally happy with him- or herself to be intimate with others. People who are honest about their self-appraisals and the intimate knowledge they develop about themselves find it helpful in relating to others. At the same time, a person who is very unhappy with him- or herself may find temporary satisfaction in relationships where someone else cares for them. Also, it is important for a person to maintain a sense of self when involved in an intimate relationship with another, and not become so preoccupied with the relationship that he or she becomes a doormat. An all-consuming relationship may be exhilarating for a short time, but it can be draining or damaging unless it evolves to a more realistic level (Masters et al. 1988).

COMMUNICATION PATTERNS

When couples bond with each other, they learn to communicate about their needs, desires, and dreams. The manner in which a person communicates varies; some people are comfortable discussing everything and others are very private.

Nobody goes into a love relationship or a marriage thinking in terms of bettering their skills or ways of communicating. People take with them what they have learned while growing up. In marital and other intimate relationships we talk about intimacy, about communication, sex, money, and various other factors. Intimacy is often misunderstood as a time and place: a table for two, with candlelight and soft music. But intimacy is more than that—it is a person's ability to talk about what he or she really is, and to say what he or she wants with a partner who listens and cares. In an intimate relationship a person can talk about his or her pain, rage, and failures. It means being able to discuss personal, social, and sexual needs, being explicit about them rather than inarticulate. A person's inability to express his or her needs or desires may cause helplessness and feelings of exploitation and anger and other problems.

> Richard was not a good communicator, and his wife, Dee, felt that through the years the communication between them had become distant, impersonal, and routine. But as Richard started to be careful about his clothes and the way he dressed, Dee became suspicious and wanted an explanation for his new attitude toward clothes. This in turn made Richard angry, as he felt that she was too demanding. He responded by not saying much and turning up the volume on the radio. In many ways his behavior

resembled that of his father, who would turn the volume to the highest level when he did not wish to listen to Richard's mother.

Janice, a newlywed, was very upset with her husband because he was not charismatic or the life of the party, not funny or a scintillating conversationalist. She had always seen her flamboyant father take over parties and be at ease while doing it. She became overly critical of her husband.

Mia was constantly criticized by her mother when she was growing up, and later identified with the mother and modeled herself after her by perpetuating the critical attitudes. Mia always felt guilty that she was not pleasing her mother, and now she began to make her husband feel the way she had felt while she was growing up. Having never felt accepted, she had a great deal of difficulty accepting her husband. In order to deal with her problems, Mia had to consciously develop new ways of responding, understand the harm that such a negative focus could bring to their relationship, and work on new ways of responding.

Thus some people carry with them unwritten agendas that they bring to the marriage from their family of origin.

When couples move simultaneously toward each other, a certain degree of attraction brings them together, often an unconscious desire to complete themselves. For example, a quiet person may be attracted to a loud person, a shy person to a boisterous one, and so on. The manner in which this attraction takes place is through communication. Body language and nonverbal and verbal behavior help people communicate with each other. In our communication patterns we also present our family patterns. All of us grow up with expectations from our parents. This is why there are different types of expectations in a marriage, but the couple may share something deeper in terms of more important similarities. Learned communication patterns are part of everyday life. All of our patterns of communication begin at home with those who are a part of our immediate environment. When a couple shares an attitude toward life, be it optimistic, pessimistic, intellectual, impulsive, or morally superior, it can unite them in binding ways.

Relationships happen through communication. Through communication we learn about approval and disapproval. By the manner in which a person speaks we receive information, through sound, touch, movement, and tone of voice. We gather meanings about ourselves and use this kind of communication with our families and others to develop a sense of our worth.

Satir and Baldwin (1983) define communication as the way people convey information, make meaning with one another, and respond internally and externally. The manner in which we communicate is the key to discerning our external and internal processes, how we handle reality, and also how much we value ourselves. As people communicate to us, even as children and infants, we begin to make interpretations of that communication that may be different from the manner in which it is intended. For example, an infant's father becomes physically disabled through an accident, and the mother is overly concerned and devotes a great deal of time to her husband. Things are not the same and the child gets less attention, less affection. The infant does not understand, but makes an assumption that the adults do not love him or her.

When people's verbal messages conflict with their nonverbal ones we call it incongruent communication. All communication carries a verbal and an affective message. For example, when a person begins to talk about something joyous but talks about it in a sad monotone, then the audience is confused, as the person's affect reveals sadness. Questions arise about what is the true message and what is the meaning of the discrepancy. When a father comes home and his wife asks, "How was your day?" and he answers "Great," with sadness, there has been an incongruent communication. In some families many messages are mixed. A child's early communication reflects incongruencies and gaps in learning. If the child embarrasses the parents, or amuses them, their reaction will provide the child with more information on rules about communication.

Examples of family rules might include:

"We do not talk about private matters to outsiders."
"Do not say anything negative about your mother."
"We do not show love except when someone does something to deserve it."
"People should understand that we love them."

In families we learn about rules by the manner in which the family gets represented. We learn rules about what we should feel, and what we may or may not say.

When we follow rules that endanger our self-esteem, we may develop physiological symptoms of illness. We learn about double levels of communication and learn to protect ourselves; basically and finally, we learn to survive. Children in some families learn not to "feel angry," and, like the iceberg, present only parts of themselves.

Thus couples come from different backgrounds and families in terms of communication patterns. Like computers, we store information about what we have processed and learned in our lives. To make sense of our life experiences, we sort them out and categorize and explain events, experiences, and ideas. The information we store comes out when we need to speak for apparent or nonapparent reasons. Growing up, we imitate our parents' ways of communicating. Depending upon how a parent communicates, we can take on a placating approach, as Satir (1982) says, "I am not all right but you are all right"; a blaming approach, where you say, "I am all right but you're not all right"; or super-reasonableness, in which the person is without emotion and is objective in his or her approach. Distractive or irrelevant communication can also affect conversations, and finally we have conversations where we can be congruent.

Every person has a need to survive, to be accepted; we often hide our desperate need to feel connected to others. The manner in which people cope depends upon how they feel about themselves. Whenever the question of mutual trust and love comes up, our survival responses come into play, based on the belief that we cannot continue living without these people (often, the family) and that their opinions and feelings always define us and our worth correctly (Satir 1982).

We are the products of our environment and in many ways we develop our sense of self-worth from different communication stances that begin very early in life. A child who is often told that he or she is not a worthy person does not feel worthy at all. Thus communication patterns begin early in life and are carried on in adult life. At times this may be a suitable way of being for some people, irrespective of whether this is functional or dysfunctional from a therapist's perspective.

> Forty-two-year-old Sarah said that she was very happy growing up. Her mother was always busy and

at age 10 Sarah took over the household work, including doing the bills and budgeting food for the family. She also took care of her sickly father, who had to undergo surgery for cancer. However, she told me in therapy, "I had a good life as a child." Thus people's reality varies, depending on what they were told and what they view as being good for them. One of Sarah's biggest problems was that she was always overly responsible at home and in her workplace, and these were the issues that needed to be worked through.

One person comes from an overly protective family and another from a home in which the child assumed a great deal of responsibility. If such a pair met and married, one could adopt the role of caretaker of the one who had been protected.

Family lifestyles and communication patterns that we learn in childhood, lifestyles that define who we are, create varying degrees of interdependence and enmeshment in our adult family situations. Each of us develops boundaries around the self and the family of origin and procreation. These boundaries define who can be included or excluded from the family, what aspects of family business—that is, secrets, family problems, and money matters—may be discussed outside the family.

There are different types of communication aggravators (Beck 1989) that contribute to negative relationships and these include coercing, coaxing, evaluating, masking, postponing, and blaming.

Coercing can be described as an attempt to crowbar your mate into submitting to your ideas or agreeing to what you say, either because of verbal commands, threats regarding the future, or even physical force. The partner may go along passively but feel embittered and angry covertly. The partner may sabotage your plans, drag his or her feet in carrying out what you need, or defy what you ask.

Coaxing is a more subtle form of coercion. In this case, you plead, beg, and try to tempt your spouse to go along with what you are doing. If your spouse perceives your manipulative efforts and becomes annoyed, he or she may refuse your wishes and become hostile.

Evaluating involves discrediting the partner's feelings or beliefs. For example, if your partner is angry with you, you may discount it by saying that perhaps the person is angry with his or her boss and taking it out on you. This might make partners more angry, as they are being asked to deny their own feelings. Another example is the wife's requesting that her husband purchase a particular item for the house, which the husband avoids doing, but when his wife expresses anger, he suggests that her feelings are related to PMS.

Masking is also called "snowing," "white lies," or "whitewashing." It involves holding back or distorting certain information. This can elicit counterefforts by the spouse to get to the truth. For example, when Martha asked, "Why were you late again last night?" George answered that he had to work late. Actually, the lateness was due to an ongoing fight between two, which George wants to avoid. What he says lacks conviction, and he wants his partner to know he is irritated with her.

Postponing is a technique in which one person delays responding to the other. When a wife asks, "When can we see my mother?" the husband rolls over in bed and responds, "I'll check my schedule," which tells the wife that he is not interested and does not wish to cooperate with her social plans. The wife picks up her husband's unenthusiastic response and gets angry. He is accused of not wanting to be part of her family.

Blaming is a common phenomenon between partners when one points a finger at the other and projects his or her own issues and problems. At times couples can be caught in a vicious cycle, where they blame each other for their problems. No solutions are ever reached, as both are indignant about each other's anger and pain, and the constant blaming puts both on the defensive.

> Dennis is a doctoral student and a father of four children. He is not able to complete his school assignments in time as his wife "distracts" him with family problems and housework. She in turn angrily retorts that he has been "neglecting the family for years." When Dennis's grades are not good, he blames it on his wife and she blames him for being an absent father and husband.

Indirectness and ambiguity is another type of communication aggravator that couples face in their relationships. When people have to communicate their thoughts, desires, and feelings with their partners, they may state their wishes in ways that obscure understanding. They may express their opinions vaguely, talk around the point, or get lost in trivial details. One partner may use too many words and the other too few. With such a communication style, both partners may feel frustration. Instead of being aware of their own contribution to the murky exchange, they blame the mate for being obtuse or bullheaded.

> Janet and Mark had lived together for three years. On the anniversary of their third year together, Mark suggested they go out to dinner. Archly, he asked, "Janet, would you like to go out for dinner tonight?" Janet, who was feeling very tired, missed the hidden

message and responded, "No, I'm tired." Mark was extremely disappointed and hurt but soon realized that he had not communicated his real desire which was to celebrate their anniversary. When he explained that to Janet, she readily agreed and they went out to celebrate.

When Otha invites his wife, Shirleen, to go to bed early, he is suggesting they make love, but Shirleen wants to watch TV. Otha is offended and then explains to her that he was thinking of lovemaking. Shirleen happily agrees to go to bed, as they start getting cozy on the living room couch.

Good communication involves getting your thoughts across and it also means understanding what the other person is saying. People who are consistently vague or indirect in their speech can lead their partners to jump to incorrect conclusions or to ignore what they say.

When a relationship has matured, partners are often able to communicate with hints and allusions, and have their own private language and idioms to carry the message. When the relationship is strained, however, the private language is no longer adequate and can promote misunderstanding.

Defensiveness is a form of communication pattern that can occur when people feel inferior. The likelihood of misunderstanding increases when they allow themselves a personal agenda, such as a desire to prove something to themselves, or to thwart rejection or ridicule, which can muddy what they are already saying. The fear of being rejected for voicing a particular opinion may increase a person's defensiveness. This often makes it difficult to decipher the hidden meanings in a person's statement.

Jerry looks at Laura and carries on this conversation:

Jerry: Are we visiting my father this weekend?
Laura: I don't think so. I've got a lot of things to do.
Jerry (*angrily*): You never really want to visit my father, do you?

In this exchange Laura took Jerry's request at face value, as simply asking her for information rather than making a request. She did not pay attention to the true meaning of Jerry's words, which was "I would like to visit my father this weekend." Jerry was wary of stating his wish outright, but was angry and reproachful when Laura refused. Behind all this is Jerry and Laura's communication style, which has ambiguities and defensiveness. Although such a relationship may create strain, there were enough strengths in the bond to absorb the strain. Both Jerry and Laura really enjoyed each other's company and therefore could discuss issues and reach compromises.

Differences in speaking styles may contribute to marital conflict. When Jack and Jean, a professional couple, made a presentation together, Jean was upset because she felt that Jack answered all the questions. She blamed him for dominating her, hogging center stage, and having no respect for her views. However, their problem was timing. Jean, who pauses for a long time between sentences, may be interrupted by Jack, who speaks more rapidly. She becomes angry because she had not completed her train of thought, and may lose track of what she wanted to say. She may accuse him of never wanting to listen to her opinions.

One way of dealing with this issue is to help the partners understand and accept their individual differences. One person might then be able to accept interruption without getting angry, knowing that the other is making a valiant effort to be a patient listener.

Deaf and blind spots also contribute to communication breakdowns and friction. This becomes apparent when one partner does not mentally register what the spouse is conveying in words, gestures, and the like. Such a lapse leads to complaints such as, "You don't know what I want or what I'm asking," or "You don't know me at all." These "spots" can be created by insensitivity or can be traced to hypersensitivity and defensiveness (Beck 1989). People often tune out what they don't want to hear, because the message may be directed toward a vulnerable area. Whenever there is a threat to their self-esteem, damage to their pride, or rejection, they set up defenses that block their view of the practical problem.

> Harold is an aggressive law professor who doesn't know how to confine his adversarial tactics to the classroom. In his relationship with his wife he puts her down, and Stephanie, a homemaker with adult children away from home, has just gone back to school to get her bachelor's degree. In social situations he ridicules her, and in private he dismisses her problems as "neurotic." When Stephanie finally got the courage to tell him she wants a divorce, he was floored. He was unaware of her misery with him and his communication style. Stephanie explained that she had stayed with him only because of the children. At this point Harold, the strong one, began to fall apart and confessed that he was unaware of the manner in which he treated her. Luckily,

after much grief and pain, they ended up in therapy, working on their individual communication patterns toward the goal of becoming caring and effective communicators. Negative communication patterns have a way of becoming vicious cycles.

BOUNDARIES

Personal Boundaries

All of us carry with us spatial boundaries that while invisible nevertheless set limits on how far we can go with comfort in a relationship (Whitfield 1993). They delineate where a person's physical and psychological space ends and where another person's begins. Paine-Gernee and Hunt (1990) say that interaction with others, family members as well as outsiders, occurs at such boundaries, that is, where you end and they begin. A good way of conceptualizing this would be to think of a boundary as a cell wall, which is a semipermeable membrane. When this cell wall functions correctly, it lets in nutrients, keeps poisons out, and excretes waste matter. The cell wall also defends the cell by separating it from other cells. Thus healthy cells know what they can include and exclude. They can also distinguish between different kinds of cells. "Healthy cells demonstrate good contact at their boundaries by discriminating between nutrition and poison and by positioning and duplicating themselves. The healthy person must do the same. To have a semipermeable membrane, to know when to allow in and when to keep out, means you have a choice in your life, and means you will be an active rather than a passive participant in it. To manage contact well is an expression of self, integrity, and freedom" (Whitfield 1933, p. 2).

A person who has clear boundaries has an awareness of who he or she is. Until a person knows that, healthy relationships, casual or intimate, will be difficult. People with healthy boundaries have a clear notion of what kinds of relationships are and are not in their own best interests. A sense of self helps a person decide which relationships to encourage because they are ego-enhancing and which to avoid as potentially destructive or toxic. Thus boundaries delineate who a person is. Boundaries also provide the protection needed to negotiate the difficult and painful junctures that people encounter in their daily lives. As people draw upon their inner resources, they can respond from their strength rather than sinking into a tired sense of worthlessness, despair, or cynicism. Understanding boundaries means understanding self: beliefs, thoughts, feelings, decisions, choices, and experiences. It means being aware of one's own wants, needs, and desires and understanding one's own sensations and thoughts. Whitfield (1993) categorizes three types of boundaries: (1) flexible, (2) boundaryless, and (3) rigid. This classification is presented for the purpose of understanding, for in reality there are no specific types of boundaries—they are different points on a continuum. Obviously, boundaries that are flexible are effective. When we use such boundaries we can be assertive without being aggressive. People with flexible boundaries can be tender, strong, firm, and respectful. Such people can dialogue in a spirit of mutual openness and discovery. Some people seem not to have any boundaries at all, and are referred to as "boundaryless," which means anyone can intrude on their space in any manner that person wishes. Often, sexually abused children fit into this category. They do not know how to ward off potential offenders, because in abuse they have learned that they do not own their own bodies. They may not know how to relate to people who are kind to them and respect their boundaries. This often happens in sexual relationships, where an abused person winds up choosing another abuser as a partner.

> Jennifer allowed anyone to talk down to her in her workplace. If people were friendly, she would take a one-down position and present a diffident self. When she met Brad, who was loving and respectful of her, she did not know how to deal with him. She could not believe that anyone would think she was worthy. She dropped Brad after the first two dates because he was too nice. Jennifer had been sexually and physically abused as a child and could not connect to people who respected her boundaries.

In quite a few marriages there is tremendous overlapping of boundaries, with crowding of people and their needs. In such families there is a great deal of enmeshment, a tremendous involvement in each other's problems and issues, and difficulty in letting go of each other and their problems. This is another form of "boundarylessness."

> Susie was a beautiful woman who always managed to get into relationships with men who used and abused her. She was overcome with shame, for intellectually she was aware that the relationships were destructive and caused her pain. She had problems discussing her family issues until she joined a group for abused women. In this group, members talked openly about their troubled family backgrounds. At this point Susie mentioned that she would be in the bathroom when her older brother

would come in an urinate in the toilet, as would her father. Family members were not allowed to close the door of the bathroom; they were told that they were shutting others out, and to be "free" with each other they had to keep all the doors open at all times. Susie said there was no privacy when she changed clothes or even took a bath. She was uncomfortable about her father and brother urinating in front of her, but did not see it as a boundary invasion until she developed awareness in the group. In many ways her boundaries had been encroached upon by her father and brother and the rest of the family members. Susie did not understand that she chose men who were also intrusive and overly demanding of her. Recalling her early family life helped to create for her some ideas about what might have happened to her sense of self and privacy with boundary invasion by important family members in her early life. For Susie this was the beginning of insight into her pattern of choosing men who were intrusive, and she began to take steps toward working on her problems.

There are also subtle boundary violations in emotional abuse that do not become clear until a child is grown up.

At a young age, Greg was told he was loved and valued, but after his sister was born, Greg felt devalued. His mother, a domineering woman, would often say, "I love my children equally." Even as a child, Greg had to do a great deal of work in the house. He cut the shrubs, mowed the lawn, and watered the plants. He vaguely observed that other boys of his age group, 6 years or so, did not do such

> chores. By the time he was 16, he was working in the family business during his school vacation time. By the time he was 21, his father had retired and Greg was in charge. Although his 15-year-old sister did not participate in any of the household chores or the business, she was made an equal partner, with equal shares in the company. While the mother continued to say that she loved her children equally, her daughter was obviously the favorite child. Greg was singled out for emotional abuse. Eventually the father died and the son was disinherited. The mother continued to say that she loved her children equally although she transferred all her property to her daughter immediately after the death of her husband. The mother was unhappy that Greg was not talking to his sister. She constantly asked him to "talk to your sister" and to be a good son and make her happy because "we are a happy family." In this family there was a total violation of boundaries and individuality.

At the other extreme are those who have overly rigid boundaries. These people focus much of their attention outside themselves. They tend to be less aware of their inner life and thus also less aware of their boundaries. Such people spend much time discussing other people's problems and keep the focus away from themselves. All problems are viewed as happening from the outside, and such people are often incapable of seeing themselves as having any type of issue or problem. Aggressively, they point their fingers at others.

> A middle-aged husband, Matt, was overly dependent upon his wife, Amber. In individual therapy Amber complained about his dependency. However, seeing them together in therapy presented a different pic-

ture. Every time Matt attempted even to pick up a pencil or get his own medicines, Amber would be at his side doing everything for him. At the same time she resented doing all the work in the house and complained to her relatives, friends, and children about his dependency. Amber grew up in a home where her mother did everything for her father and Amber believed that that was how a wife should be. However, she found pleasure in telling her near and dear ones how dependent her husband was, just like her mother used to do. When she was made aware of this in therapy, she was totally distraught, thinking that there was a conspiracy to make her look bad, because he needed her and she was a "good wife." When Matt finally got the courage to say that he could begin to do things to help her, she quickly hushed him by saying, "You know you can't, you have to work in your office all day long." In a manipulative way she was gaining the sympathy of her children although, rigidly, her own agenda was not to allow her husband to work in the house. There was apparently no respect for other people's spaces, and Amber constantly crowded her husband's boundaries with her own rigidity, and had little respect for his uniqueness or individuality.

People are complex and weave a life that is comfortable for them, and often follow the rules developed in their family of origin unless they make special efforts to change.

Understanding boundaries helps us discover how to develop genuine intimacy. We learn to set limits regarding the unacceptable behaviors of others, and also discover core issues that lead us to ignore and overlook our actual experiences. Awareness of boundaries helps us discover past wounds that may prevent us from standing up to present mistreatment.

PURSUER AND DISTANCER STYLES

In relationships between dominant and subordinate groups, the subordinate group members always possess greater understanding of the dominant groups and their culture than vice versa. Similarly in marriages, the submissive partner begins to understand the domineering partner better through the years. However, before any partner becomes the domineering partner, there is a power struggle as each person tries to find his or her place in the marriage or relationship.

> Christina was in love with Jeff, and his former girlfriend called Christina to warn her that Jeff has a bad temper and is a woman-beater. Christina, who believed in Jeff, and who had seen his outstanding qualities as a professional athlete and a socialite, overlooked his former girlfriend's warning and put it down to jealousy. However, after they had been in the relationship for six months they got into an argument and he pushed her around until she began to feel afraid, as she was no match for his tall athletic frame. Within half an hour he was the same loving man she had met a few months before, so Christina rationalized and believed that he had had a "bad day," an explanation that Jeff offered her. There were two more such incidents and each time Christina forgave him. Soon they got married, and life changed dramatically for Christina as she realized that he was an abusive man who beat her frequently. The power situation changed in the marital relationship as Christina, who was in the

subordinate role, began to understand Jeff's every mood and to expect mistreatment whenever he flew off the handle. She was too afraid to leave the relationship, as he threatened her with death, suicide, and other such blackmail. Christina, with fear, began to distance herself, but when Jeff was not satisfied with her explanations he became the relentless pursuer, questioning her about everything until she was no longer able to give him "the perfect answer." At this point he attacked her physically. Christina was aware of her fearful distancing, but was also aware that she did not have a way out of this trapped, abusive marriage.

In our culture we usually learn to handle anxiety in one of two ways: by pursuing or distancing (Lerner 1989).

Pursuers reduce or manage anxiety by getting close to the other person. They want to resolve everything by talking about feelings, perceptions, problems, and situations that create anxiety. They want to resolve emotional issues quickly, so that issues that obstruct closeness will not create any more anxiety for them. Pursuers usually handle anxiety in this manner when they are close to a significant other. The *overexpressive mate* is the pursuer who wants to discuss everything in detail and wants answers to all questions, or at least a discussion. Some tend to pursue to the point of exasperation as they get no response; this often ends in their expressing their anger loudly and repeatedly. A few of them live in a whirlwind of emotional frenzy and feel uncomfortable when everything appears to be all right. Basically, the pursuer is looking for good communication as well as reasonable emotional attachment with the spouse, but this does not seem to happen.

Distancers function differently; they handle anxiety

in the opposite fashion. They hesitate to discuss what bothers them. They distance themselves from significant others, preferring to manage emotional issues by themselves. Distancers tend not to express feelings, thoughts, problems, and perceptions. When they are pressured to speak, their anxiety increases. The more the pursuer follows, the more the distancer attempts to keep away.

> I saw a couple in therapy where the wife wished to have more closeness with her husband. She said she has heard "I love you" from him only once a year, although he was very loving and affectionate while they were dating. When this was brought up before the husband, he remarked with irritation, "I married her, didn't I? Why should I keep telling her that I love her all the time? She should know that."

Being a pursuer or a distancer has an effect on marriage, but all human behavior is varied and complicated, and the categories of pursuer and distancer (and overfunctioning and underfunctioning people, which will be discussed later) are the ends of a continuum and are not mutually exclusive.

Being a pursuer or a distancer can create problems. The impact of these communication styles has an effect on couples.

> A 44-year-old woman, Cindy, is in her second marriage to her teacher and professor, Rick. After four years of marriage, she experiences coldness, aloofness, and secretiveness in her spouse, which really bothers her. When asked how the dating progressed, she said that they had known each other for ten years before they married. Cindy had known Rick while she was married to her first husband and they

had all been friends. She could confide in Rick about all her marital issues, and when her marriage turned bitter she turned to Rick for support and help. He offered everything she needed wholeheartedly, and ultimately married her. Rick is five years younger than Cindy and has suddenly "shut down." I see both of them in therapy, separately at this point, as they have a number of issues they need to work out in their personal lives in terms of their families of origin. Rick is rigid, and does not like to "waste unnecessary words" with his wife. He has maintained all his friendships with women, but will not allow her to maintain her own friendships with men. Women call him at home at any time of day or night and he carries on conversations for two hours, but will not tolerate his wife's doing the same. Because Cindy was his student, he has to be better at everything. He still treats her like a student. In Rick's defense, he was not aware of this pattern but today is working at moving away from it. Cindy complains that when she tries to talk to him he shuts down and will not respond to her, except sarcastically, which Cindy experiences as a put-down. He is not loving, and pulls away from her when she tries to be affectionate. He complains that she should know that he loves her. She on the other hand feels alone and unloved and wishes to hear something loving every day or, as she specified, "every other day." Often when she talks and tries to help him communicate she ends up feeling like a "fool." She gets angry and "rants and raves" and he immediately leaves the home and shuts down for a much longer period. She added, "I never know what is going on in his mind." Rick said in therapy, "My biggest problem is learn-

> ing not to keep everything to myself and allowing my wife to be part of my inner feelings. I found out she doesn't have a magic wand and doesn't automatically understand how I feel."

Often members in pursuer–distancer, man–woman, husband–wife relationships reach an impasse with each other. The challenge in such relationships is that when a relationship becomes a source of negative energy and frustration, attempts to fix it can lead to more of the same, creating defensiveness, fear of losing control, and much anger. These "stuck" relationships can be too intense or too distant. Too much intensity means that one person is overfocused on the other and is blaming or worried about that person all the time. The person overfocused on someone else tends to be underfocused on self. Once a relationship becomes stuck, it is difficult to bring about changes, as both partners are reacting with strong feelings and their positions may become polarized. When there is significant intensity, we react rather than observe and think. When we overfocus on another person we tend to see only one side of the situation, our own, and are unable to see the other person's point of view. There is a great deal of anxiety in such a situation. We may have a strong wish for change and be unaware of the actual sources of anxiety that are affecting our relationships. Often we are fueling the relationship problem and overlooking or blocking intimacy (Lerner 1989).

In unhealthy marriages the inevitable life stressors unbalance the relationship. Some people may resort to over- and underfunctioning behaviors in order to manage the resultant anxiety and to restore their own equilibrium (Kerr and Bowen 1988, Lerner 1989). As long as their relationships and roles are flexible, balance can be restored. Often in couples who come into therapy, these roles have become rigid, and one person always plays the overfunctioning partner and the other the underfunctioning partner. Overfunctioning and underfunctioning can create serious problems in marriages.

> Randy and Melissa were engaged, and during the time of their engagement Melissa gladly took care of Randy's needs. After marriage and six children, Melissa was still doing the same thing. They both occupied rigid roles. He was the typical underfunctioner and she was the overfunctioner. Randy rationalized that his job kept him away from home and domestic responsibilities; therefore he did very little around the house. After work he would sit in the family room watching TV or play golf with his friends. Melissa took up the slack and did almost everything in the house. She was the primary caretaker of their six children, which included driving them to the doctor, their music classes, and athletic practices; checking their homework assignments; overseeing and helping them participate in household chores; helping them shop for school clothes; and so forth. Melissa also did the cooking and cleaning and took care of Randy's clothes and dishes that he left in different rooms. In addition, Melissa had a full-time job. Nothing Melissa said or did would make Randy change his position on how the family duties should be divided. After seventeen years of miserable power struggles, Melissa became chronically angry and admitted that her husband was a burden and that she did not love him at all. Although Melissa blamed Randy for the failure of their marriage, both had unwittingly contributed to it. By being mutually reinforcing and creating a

rigid pattern that prevailed through a number of years, they both contributed to their marital conflicts. Finally, Melissa in disgust and anger left the marriage.

All of us go through painful times in our relationships and talk about wanting a change. However, when there are both a pursuer and a distancer in the marriage, there is often a need to look at unaddressed issues, present and past, and begin to deal with them.

To be in a good relationship requires a certain degree of mature intimacy, which has to do with dealing with self before we deal with others. In distancing, either one or both of the partners move away and do not deal with their own issues. When someone uses distancing with a partner, it becomes a way of avoiding issues. Lerner (1989) indicates that this becomes the primary way of dealing with intensity in key relationships, including the ones in our family of origin. Moving to another area or state to avoid face-to-face contact with relatives is one example of our ways of maintaining distance.

Katherine disinherited her only son, Jim, who had been a provider for the family. When she called him after three months, she pretended that nothing had happened. She talked as if there had been no estrangement. She asked him what he wanted for Christmas, and mentioned that she missed his wife and her son. When Jim asked her why she was calling him after disinheriting him, she replied that she did not remember disinheriting him and added that she had not done anything wrong. Although she was talking to him, there was a total absence of real warmth or understanding, and the whole conversation was aimed at making herself feel good. She was a toxic parent, concerned only about her own feelings and well-being, and an emotional distancer.

When people have difficulty with intimacy, they may move forward or drift backwards in their relationships.

Bill and Becky were weighed down with problems. Becky gave birth to a baby and was overly involved with her son, while her husband stayed away from home and spent more time in the office. Meanwhile, Becky's father became ill with lung cancer. He was very old and feeble and the cancer advanced rapidly. Although he complained of pain, the cancer was kept a secret. Becky discussed all her fears and pain with her mother but acted as if everything was all right in front of her father. Meanwhile, Bill was becoming distanced in their marital relationship, and finally had an emotional fling with a woman in his office. As soon as she knew that her husband was having an affair, Becky went to work on her marriage. Bill was not ready for intimacy with her. She pursued him, insisting that he talk about everything with her. The more she pursued him, the more he distanced himself. Concurrently, Becky avoided her own issues with her father and also her brother, Brandon, with whom she had not spoken in years. As therapy progressed, she began to talk to her father about his cancer and her feelings concerning his death and its impact on her. She saw herself having no relationship with her brother, but found that she did care about him. She recognized that her distancing from him had started when he began doing drugs. Similar to and in support of her mother, who was angry with Brandon, Becky became overly anxious and angry and kept away from her brother. In therapy, Becky began to look at herself and her issues. It began to dawn on her that there was a longstanding pattern of distancing in her family of origin. When serious issues had to be discussed, the family members withdrew and pretended the issues did not exist. Becky did the same in her marriage until the crisis of an affair made her look at herself and her issues with herself, her parents, her brother, and her husband. As Becky grew in therapy, she became more aware and paid more attention to herself, and was less reactive to Bill's every move. Becky realized that she could not achieve her goal of closeness with Bill by staying narrowly fixed on her marriage.

In a paradoxical sense, couples become less able to achieve intimacy if they stay focused on it and give it their total attention. Real closeness occurs most reliably when it is not pursued or demanded in a relationship but when both individuals work consistently on themselves. As Lerner (1989) indicates, working on oneself means clarifying beliefs, values, and life goals, and becoming responsible, defining the "I" in key relationships, and addressing important emotional issues as they arise.

The pursuer and distancer styles also become a negative struggle when partners use them as a personal style of arguing and as a power tool. They may clash more often when they do not have a common understanding between them. Instead of being able to come to mutual decisions and successfully resolve issues, the couple may spend a great deal of time together attacking each other on how to communicate.

Alicia spoke of her husband: "How do my husband and I resolve problems? Usually I start a discussion, and it ends up as a monologue. We never discuss anything. By the end of it, I'm always shouting that he is not part of it and, worse still, there are no responses at all. At this point I become annoyed and begin to yell and scream, for I feel like I'm talking to a wall. Quietly, he responds that I'm always shouting and not talking."

The irony of the pursuer–distancer conflict is that one partner craves a close relationship whereas the other fears or is uncomfortable with the closeness and tries to move away. The more the pursuer chases, the more the distancer moves away emotionally, which leaves the pursuer feeling left out and alone in his or her need, desire, and misery. As one client mentioned, "He never puts his arms around me, ever, and I always feel alone and left out. I feel a coldness all the time."

Eventually all communication becomes a major argument in which two people feel embittered with each other, feel hopeless, and never come to a resolution. Such fights between couples may be characterized by screaming and yelling or by the silent treatment. During these vicious cycles arguments can continue to snowball rather than come to an end. The frustrated partners cannot communicate but only spin circles around each other.

As Beck (1989) indicates, this is how a vicious cycle works. You have a disagreement, and this leads to your feeling attacked, threatened, hurt, uncared for, unloved, or berated, which sets the cycle in motion. After a disagreement between two people, the injured or offended party may withdraw and set another negative pattern in motion, which might involve grudge-holding, delayed explosion, a vengeful attitude, or an inducement of guilt.

During these embittered battles you may be surprised at your own anger and also at the anger your spouse presents. You may say or do startling things to each other.

> In therapy, one man complained that when he was dating his present wife she was mild-mannered and affectionate and did not appear to have a temper, although they had dated for two years. One day, when they got into a who-will-win fight, he was taken by surprise when his wife started to scratch him and leave bloody nail marks all over him. She supported him, saying, "I am scared of my own rage."

Why do such vicious battles happen in a marriage? Often it is because there are many incidents or behaviors that one of the partners was not expecting.

> Scott married Amanda because she was quiet, timid, and shy, and these qualities were appealing to him. They dated for two-and-a-half years and also managed to get away together on weekends. However, two months into their marriage, Amanda was annoyed at her husband for not being punctual. When he came later than the specified time, she flew into a temper tantrum and threw their spaghetti dinner at the kitchen wall while screaming, cursing, and yelling at him. Scott was shocked—this was not the woman he had married. He dreaded women with bad tempers and had not seen this type of behavior in Amanda while they were dating. In anger, pain, and fear, Scott shut down completely, thus creating the scenario of pursuer and distancer in their marriage.

GENDER DIFFERENCES

Another reason for disparity among couples is the different styles in which men and women relate to each other. Allowing for individual differences, women tend to be relationship-oriented, whereas men tend to be more task-oriented. However, no one should overwork or feel compelled to take care of everyone else in the family. Lerner (1989), in discussing male–female relationships, says that an intimate relationship is one in which neither party silences, sacrifices, or betrays the self and each party expresses strength and vulnerability, weakness and competence, in a balanced manner. Maltz and Borker (1982) summarize a number of findings that shed light on why marital partners have problems communicating. One reason is that men and women have different conversational styles. Although the couples may have essentially the same style, in many instances there is a difference in communication, with the wife adopting a culturally defined "feminine" conversational style and the husband a "masculine" style. As Beck (1989) puts it, women characteristically show a greater tendency to ask questions and, in observations of female–male conversations, a question and answer pattern was found, with females asking most of the questions. Research has indicated that women maintain routine interactions through questioning. Their questioning is a sign that they take responsibility for facilitating and sustaining the flow of conversation. This conversational device suggests greater involvement in personal relations, and contrasts with men, who are less likely to ask personal questions. Men are prone to think, "If she wants to tell me, she'll tell me without asking." A woman will think, "If I don't ask, he'll think that I don't care." Men may think of questions as intrusive meddling, and an invasion of privacy, whereas women see them as a show of intimacy and an expression of caring.

Beck (1989) also observed that: (1) men are more likely to interrupt their conversational partners, either male or female; (2) men are less likely to respond to comments of the other speaker—frequently they make no response or acknowledgment at all, or give a delayed response at the end of their partner's statement, which shows a minimum degree of enthusiasm; (3) men are more likely to challenge or dispute statements made by their partners, which explains why a husband may seem to be eternally argumentative; and (4) men make more declarations of fact or opinion than do women.

A number of wives resent the voice of authority that a husband uses, not realizing that a husband's assertions may represent a masculine style of communication rather than an attitude of superiority. A woman may view her husband as being uninterested, controlling, or unresponsive when his way of speaking simply reflects the style he has learned to use with everyone, not just with her. Women make judgments, such as "My husband disagrees with everything I say," although it more often reflects the husband's habits of speech rather than any insensitivity or ill will toward his wife. Being aware that such differences exist and that they are not caused by bad faith, lack of respect, or lack of interest can help couples to note each partner's style without taking offense, and to provide a safeguard against misinterpretation.

Although it may be tempting to attribute the differences in conversational styles to asymmetrical power relationships between men and women, and to the existence of personality differences between them, there are other explanations. In conversational styles it appears that men and women belong to different subcultures. Maltz and Borker (1982) point out that there are highly specific differences between men and women in their concept of friendly conversations, their rules for engaging in conversation, and their rules for interpreting what the partner is saying, because they learn to communicate differently from childhood due to the influence of culture. As Maltz and Borker indicate, systematic observations of boys and girls reveal that girls learn to give support and let others speak and to acknowledge what other girls say as a way of maintaining relationships of equality and closeness. For girls, talking represents a bridge and a binding force. Girls form friendships through talking and sharing secrets. Girls are much freer in discussing their feelings, which include love, hate, anxiety, and sadness. Girls' friendships are formed through conversations. Girls tend to criticize and argue with other girls who are perceived to be "bossy" or "mean." They are less likely to order people around, and believe in the concept of equality. Shifting alliances within girls' small peer groups makes them pay more attention to reading the intent of other girls. Thus, in many ways, girls become increasingly sophisticated in discerning one another's motives, detecting nuances, and interpreting what people mean.

Boys, on the other hand, play in large organized groups, and these groups place a high premium on status and dominance. Boys who have relatively low status in groups are made to feel inferior because of their status position. The social world of boys, unlike that of girls, consists of posturing, asserting dominance, and trying to command the attention of an audience. They are also inclined to threats or boasts, such as "If you don't shut up, I will shut you up forever." They tend to be more argumentative than girls. Girls tend to use words to bridge their relationships and build them, whereas boys use words as weapons of dominance. The most powerful boy in the group is not the aggressive one, but the one who is more effective and skillful in his speech. A boy's conversation revolves around dominance and aggressiveness, while a girl looks for intimacy and equality. When it comes to creating an intimate relationship, boys and girls, men and women, view it differently. Gray (1992) indicates that men are like rubber bands: in intimate relationships they often have to pull away, but they can stretch only so far before they come springing back. Gray says that a rubber band is a perfect metaphor for understanding the male intimacy cycle. This cycle involves getting close, pulling away, then getting close again. Of course, a man may also pull away for the same reasons a woman pulls away, because he is angry with her and does not trust her. However, a woman pulls away only because she does not trust him to understand her feelings, when she is hurt and afraid of being hurt again, or when he does something wrong or disappoints her. A man pulls away because he needs to fulfill his need for independence or autonomy. When he has fully stretched he will come back again, all on his own. When he has fully separated he will feel the need for love and intimacy again, and he will be motivated to give his love and receive the love he needs. When a man springs back, he picks up the relationship at whatever level of intimacy it was when he stretched away. He does not feel the need to get reacquainted. A woman in a relationship who does not understand a man's need for intimacy and autonomy at different intervals may feel that he does not love her or that his emotional distancing occurs because she did something to offend him. When a woman sees the emotional distancing, she may respond with "Let's talk" when he wants to be left alone. This commonly leads women to say, "Every time I talk, he pulls away and I feel that he doesn't care about me." However, if a woman gives a man "time out" when he does not wish to communicate, he can return with the same or a higher degree of love and caring, as is common in men's intimacy cycle. In growing up, expectations of men in intimate relationships are not as demanding. Women tend to settle for small changes in a relationship and tolerate behaviors in men that they would not tolerate from women. This is encouraged from very young childhood, when parents expect that "boys will be boys." Daughters learn about communication and responsible connectedness. Until recently, in many homes, there was respect toward the father as the authority figure. As I once heard my father say, "I wonder how it was that my father became a hero to me but my mother did not become the heroine, although she did all the taking care of. I did not recognize her strength."

Men are frequently at a loss about how to become experts on close relationships, although their anxiety may be masked by apparent apathy or disinterest. Men raised by fathers who were conspicuous by their emotional or physical absence were men ruled by their omnipotent mothers, whose feminine qualities they were taught to repudiate in themselves. The old definition of family hardly provided a good training ground for developing a clear male self in the context of emotional connectedness to others. Men who face too many problems with a partner may often distance themselves or break away from the relationship and develop a new one with similar expectations. If the second partner is also demanding in terms of intimacy, the man may become confused and find fault with the woman rather than look at himself and his own issues in terms of intimacy. These attitudes get transmitted to the next generation.

Often there are problems between couples because it is difficult to be intimate with someone with whom you disagree much of the time. Problems arise because we view our reality as the only reality and would be comfortable if everyone felt, reacted, and worked exactly the same way we do. We may confuse closeness with sameness, and may view human intimacy as the merging of two separate "I's" into a single world view. However, the fact is that we are different and we all see the world through different lenses. The world can become very different when we view it through the filters of age, race, gender, ethnic background, family background, social class, and sibling position. There are differences in values, beliefs, priorities, and habits, and also differences in how we manage anxiety and navigate under stress. Unless we understand and accept our male and female differences, it is difficult, if not impossible, to focus and build upon the common ground.

> Mary was living with David until he got a new job and moved to a different area. Mary became anxious and wanted to get married or get a serious commitment from him, which she did not get. The more he avoided a commitment, the more anxious she got. Her anxiety was exacerbated by the terminal illness of her father. The more she needed support and reassurance from her lover, the less she got. He said he would need at least two years to work out his own plans before he could think of a commitment. Finally Mary realized that she was pursuing a man who did not wish to be pursued. She also became aware of her own pattern. All her anxiety and anger at David for not making a commitment made her so anxious that she could not concentrate on her own issues of growing up. Her highest priority, until David began seriously to put her off, was to ensure that the relationship did not fail. After weeks and months of agonizing, Mary realized that she was

putting too much effort into the relationship and overlooking her own needs. She was neglecting her work and paying very little attention to her own goals. She realized that her focus on the relationship was becoming an obsession. Finally Mary realized that in order to live with herself she had to work on her own self and her own issues, including her father's terminal illness. Focusing on self is an extremely important aspect of growing up and becoming a person. This case had a happy ending when David decided, after he had lived by himself for a few months, that he wanted to marry Mary. By this time, Mary had looked at her own issues and was ready for a commitment out of love rather than insecurity and fears. The two of them did get married and both appeared to be confident that they had made the right decision.

For both men and women, achievement of happy, long-lasting, growth-enhancing relationships requires attention to one's own goals and communication patterns as well as sensitivity to the needs and feelings of colleagues, friends, lovers, and spouses.

CHAPTER THREE

Lack of Intimacy and Deviant Sexual Behaviors in the Family

A GROWING BODY OF KNOWLEDGE reveals that intimacy promotes human well-being and its absence has deleterious effects on family members. According to Prager (1995), in comparison to people who have intimate relationships, those who do not have higher mortality rates, more accidents, and higher risks of developing illness. People who do not have intimate relationships also suffer more from loneliness and develop more symptoms of psychological disturbance.

Intimacy involves interactions, experiences, and relationships. Intimate interactions are communicative exchanges between people. This involves a personal sharing of the self, and sharing includes both verbal and nonverbal elements. Verbal sharing, as discussed earlier, is self-disclosure with empathy and support from the listener. It includes verbalization of emotions and thoughts. Nonverbal sharing includes touching, shared emotional expressions, and sexual activity with partners. Sharing the self means sharing vulnerable aspects of the self. Intimate experiences are the feelings and thoughts that people have as a result of intimate interactions. Intimate relationships are a series of interactions between two individuals who are known to each other; this relationship is affected by past interactions and is also likely to influence future interactions.

Nonverbal intimacy involves maintaining forward-leaning eye contact and close physical proximity when people are interacting. Intimacy involves the effective and cognitive/perceptual components of an individual's involvement or interest in the interaction with another.

> Louise and Charles had a cozy, comfortable dinner with some close friends; while returning home, they held hands, off and on, while Charles was driving the car, and gave each other warm intimate looks that felt positive for both of them. Occasionally they spoke about their friends and what that friendship meant for them.

> Angela and Starling are returning from visiting friends. Angela is angry and accuses Star of flirting with the hostess. She calls the hostess a number of ugly names while Star angrily defends the hostess and finally ends up calling his wife some ugly names. Although the couple is having a heated argument and being open about their feelings, there is no intimacy here, but rather mistrust, anger, and pain.

As discussed earlier, people learn about intimacy, communication, and togetherness while growing up in families. The family culture, as well as the societal culture, has an effect on how family members relate to each other. If children grow up in a family where the family theme is "We are a happy family," the family will view itself as devoid of family problems. In such families, intimacy is a threat and open, honest conversations are avoided. In some families, the overworked mother avoids any kind of intimacy with her husband, as their verbal communications lead to physical fighting, and therefore they create distance between them. The parents communicate to each other through a particular child, who often becomes the burden bearer. When there is a lack of emotional intimacy, sexual interaction may proceed routinely to satisfy physical needs, or may be viewed as a burden to be tolerated or avoided.

ROLE OF CULTURAL FACTORS IN SEXUALITY

While sexuality is part of our human nature, the way we feel, think, and act in this area is definitely culture-bound. Contemporary North American culture is characterized by a clash of values or norms in this area, with the values of sexual openness and freedom coming into conflict with the political definition of morality rooted in our religious heritage. For example, breastfeeding is prohibited in most public places because it is considered indecent or improper. Why? Because the breast is seen as a sex object, although the function of the breast is to breastfeed a newborn child. Many other countries do not share our inhibitions in this area. Nudity is another issue in which the unclothed body is seen as indecent and sexually provocative. Erotic magazines are bought by young and older people in secrecy to satisfy their sexual needs. In a number of European countries, being unclothed at a beach is considered quite acceptable. However, we cannot do this in our culture because we may get arrested. Nudity is not accepted except in magazines or art and in the movies. This is not true of many other countries. In India, for example, the temples have carvings that depict sexual postures and nudity as natural happenings. Most children grow up touching these erotic sculptures and viewing the depiction of sexuality as a natural life phenomenon, not as vulgar or bad. American tourists, however, busily take photos, as this overt sexuality is unusual and unnatural to us. We may advocate the Puritan ethic but promote sexuality, explicitly and implicitly, in our proper culture. A particularly virulent form of sexual exploitation is child pornography, because it victimizes children as it caters to prurient interests of immature or disturbed adults.

Often we do not offer straight and simple answers to children's questions about sexuality. Some parents take the position that they should give all the details of how babies are made. When an answer is laborious and technical, it only confuses a child. Answers should suit the age and maturity of the child. Explaining matters in a way that makes sense to them, rather than boring or confusing them with details or answering them with half-truths, should satisfy a child's needs.

Some parents view and treat children's sexual parts as something to be ashamed of, particularly those parents who identify the private parts by other than their real names. One mother said that her daughter was "touching *there* . . . the dirty part."Another mother in therapy had been taught to call her parts "peanut, buttercup," and on. This does not make sex organs more attractive but only creates in the child a feeling that talking about "it" is forbidden. Sexual misinformation frequently begins at home, with devastating consequences.

In the beginning of the academic year, Emily's kindergarten teacher realized that the little girl thought that she was a boy. She always referred to herself as a boy and adopted the male role in all dramatic play activities. She became very angry when other children told her she was a girl, not a boy. She shouted, "I'm a boy! Why don't you believe me?" During the first parent–teacher conference after school began, the teacher asked the parents if they were concerned that Emily thought she was a boy. The parents admitted that they were quite concerned because they thought their little girl would stop pretending to be a boy after school started. The parents said they realized now that she was not pretending and often claimed she could do many activities at school better than any of the girls because she was a boy. The mother revealed that Emily refused to wear any of her girl's clothes, including under- or outer garments. After a puzzling discussion, the parents confessed that they had created the situation and were responsible for Emily's self-deception. They mentioned that they had had a young son who died when he was only a week old. The mother, in mourning, had continually called Emily her "little boy" and called her "Johnny" for two full years. She said this manner of dealing with her loss had kept her from a nervous breakdown. The father was aware of this behavior but was more concerned about his wife's health and did not pay any attention to the child. The teacher was also told that Emily wore her dead brother's new clothing until she was 2 years old. The parents said that this was for economic reasons but later accepted the explanation that they were trying to replace their lost son through Emily. It was only recently that they began to realize the trauma that Emily had suffered in terms of her own sexual identity. They asked for professional referrals so that they could all undergo counseling.

The deception that Emily experienced was especially destructive, as she became confused about her own sexual identity and gender role in the classroom and in society. She was victimized unknowingly by parents who were mourning the loss of a son and used her to overcome their own guilt and loss. Their nonchalant attitude about her sexual identity, until it became a serious issue in the school, did not seem to bother them. Imagine some of the serious issues that Emily is likely to face if all her confusions about her own sexual and personal identity are not promptly worked through in therapy.

Other children have been victims of adult abuse in more serious ways. An adult survivor of childhood incest, who was called "Angel" and "Princess," and who had been in therapy for a long period of time said, "I can feel overwhelmed with hurt and confusion. I can feel how painful it was to enjoy something that was mentally and emotionally repugnant" (Maltz and Holman 1987, p. 77). Commonly, there is a lifetime of hurt, anger, and confusion that may be helped through therapy.

Another woman who was abused from childhood to young adulthood by her father, stepfather, brother, and uncle explained in agony:

> *I thought I'd be blamed and shamed. I had a crush on my stepfather, so I thought I caused the incest at age 5. He reinforced my thinking. As I grew older, I had a great number of unfounded*

> *fears, such as that my mother would have a nervous breakdown or kill someone, or that some unknown and horrible shameful catastrophe would happen. We were not emotionally close. I created my fantasy world for survival. . . . I was always under extreme stress. I felt suicidal, and at times homicidal. I wished I could kill my stepfather. I was barely on the edge of sanity.*

Children who have been sexually abused have a number of issues to deal with, and anger is one of them. Often their anger is displaced onto others in self-destructive ways.

> Barbara would talk in derogatory ways in front of her boss and office colleagues, and would get upset with anyone who interfered in her way of doing things. For instance, she screamed at a police officer for pulling her over because she was speeding. Her cursing at him got her into even more trouble.

> Taralene saw herself as stupid, bad, ugly, shameful, and inherently worthless, but she did not share an important secret that drained all her energies—she was sexually, physically, and emotionally abused throughout her childhood and early adolescence.
>
> Taralene and her identical twin sister were conceived during their mother's affair with a friend's husband. The mother committed suicide when the twins were 4, and they were sent to live with their father and stepmother/friend. From the time of their arrival, the girls were repeatedly told that they were the cause of their mother's suicide. Their stepmother hit them, dunked them in tubs of cold water

(particularly during a cold day), pushed them down flights of stairs, called them abusive and insulting names, and made them stand in the corner for hours with wet clothes around their heads. Their father, who often traveled on business, was jolly and affectionate, but sexually molested both girls, although neither knew of their father's activities with the other.

Taralene realized in long-term therapy that it was the abuse and the acts of abuse rather than she who was repulsive. A great deal of work was done to enhance her self-esteem. She was helped to develop admiration and respect for herself for surviving the terrible family situation and being able to get an education and marry.

Abuse of a child in a family or origin, be it emotional, verbal, physical, or sexual, can create barriers to forming intimate relationships, because the hurt and pain of rejection that such children faced growing up overwhelms them. Without therapeutic help, many of these people cannot move forward in their own lives.

TRUST ISSUES

Trust begins when a parent feeds, cleans, and cuddles a child. Trust is a delicate phenomenon that underlies every aspect of a child's emotional development. A child born into a family learns to understand the dynamics of the family even as an infant. Some infants learn that they can cry all day long but nobody is going to come in to feed them. Others fear the touch of a hand because if they cry (and often they cannot help it) they will be spanked. Others learn about abuse at a young age. Many infants are enthusiastic because they quickly recognize that they will be fed, fussed about, and cuddled. We all grow up with images of what we experienced and shaped us as individuals. A child who grew up with no compliments does not know how to give or take one. When the family becomes the place where everything is stressful, the child grows up being stressed. Many children (and later adults) come from homes where fear, shame, and pain are a normal phenomenon. As a young member of a family, children do not have permission to leave and would not know how to do it. For some children, home after school is stress. The mother may be an alcoholic, or the father an abusive person. Children learn to tolerate and also become shaped by what they see, feel, and experience. As one 30-year-old told me, "I was afraid of my father. He would come home every evening in a really bad mood and would want dinner, hot and right on the table. . . . If there was a delay of a few minutes he would create a scene. His most common way of showing anger was by using us children to show my mother that he had power over her through us. He would lift us up with one hand around our necks to the point we would feel we were being choked or he would pull us up by our hair and when we cried he would tell Mom she was responsible, as dinner was not ready. We were all afraid of dinner time. . . . I still am, I cannot relax in the evenings before dinner and would be afraid to live with a man and trust him and serve him dinner."A sad lesson in lack of intimacy and, of course, abuse, leading to feelings of mistrust.

For people, even for children, to remain in relationships and to create new ones, trust is an important ingredient. As Erikson (1963) indicated, basic trust starts to develop out of a child's experiences with major figures in the family. The trust goes beyond the blind dependency of infancy and springs from a child's feelings about his parents and siblings. It includes themes such as (1) I can count on my family when I need them; (2) outsiders may hurt me but my family respects me and will protect me; and (3) important people in my life will not overstep their bounds and take advantage of me and knowingly injure me. Trust is an important ingredient in a rewarding and successful relationship (Fehr 1988).

Trust is the fundamental component of all important social relationships. Trust in a close relationship means having a level of confidence in another person in terms of the different ways he or she will act to fulfill expectations. Trust grows out of the basic human capacity to develop goals and make plans for the future. Trusting another human being means giving that person some control over events, with the confidence that rejection or betrayal will not occur. The foundation of trust is established in the earliest relationships with parents. In his theory of human development Erikson (1963) theorizes that the critical developmental task or crisis to be confronted in the first year of life is that of trust versus mistrust. Trust in infancy sets the foundation for a lifelong expectation that the world will be a safe and pleasant place to live. This idea is shared by Bowlby (1973) and Ainsworth and her colleagues (1978). These writers and theorists hypothesize that infants share a biological drive to form an attachment with a caregiver in order to achieve a feeling of security and a sense of comfort. The quality of the attachment depends upon the nature of the interactions that the infants have had with their chief caretakers in the first year of life. If the caregivers are sensitive and responsive to the child, the infants will develop a secure sense of attachment and believe they are worthy of being cared for and having their needs met. However, if children are responded to inconsistently and sporadically, then they may develop an insecure attachment to people. They may view the world as hostile or unreliable, and this is the beginning of lack of trust.

When adults create trusting relationships, they begin to take risks and indicate that they are willing to set their own interests aside as they take their partner's concerns into account, expecting that their partner will do the same. Whenever there are successful experiences of disclosure or conflict resolution, there is further evidence of the partner's commitment to the relationship and greater confidence that the relationship will be fulfilling. In relationships, as well as in marriages, trust is not created and left to grow unaided; trust is a dynamic process. Even when a solid foundation of trust has been established, levels of confidence go up and down in response to changes and transitions in the relationship. Just as trust can be built up, it can also wear down or be torn down. The relationships of people with a high degree of trust are categorically different from the relationships of people whose trust levels are lower (Rempel 1995).

Trust relationships can be classified into: (1) high-trust, (2) medium-trust, and (3) low-trust (Rempel 1995). The beliefs of high-trust people are anchored both by positive conclusions about their partner's motives based upon past evidence and by faith in what the future holds.

> When Clayton went to work at a summer camp for young adolescent girls, his wife was comfortable and completely at ease. Although she had the choice of going up to see him every evening, she avoided doing that as she wanted him to be aware that she trusted and respected him.

In medium-trust relationships people are uncertain about their partner's intentions. They have been hurt before, and develop a pattern of continuing to look for signs that indicate further risk. They still have hopes in their relationship and wish to achieve a sense of security that seems to be missing.

> Jonathon and Jenny were married and in their early twenties. Jenny's former boyfriend had had an affair, which created a number of issues for Jenny in her present relationship. So when Jonathon was asked to take care of teenage girls at a summer camp, Jenny made it her business to spy on her husband and visit him as often as she could. Although she made a nuisance of herself, she was clear that she had to do everything to reassure herself that everything was fine in the marriage and her husband was "in control of himself and his emotions" in the summer camp. Jenny was not disappointed.

In low-trust relationships people have taken risks and lost. The sad irony is that once trust has been betrayed, it may be overwhelmingly difficult to restore. Even if the unfaithful partner turns over a new leaf and begins to work on the relationship, it is very easy for the betrayed partner to explain away these positive behaviors. There is always the possibility of further deception and disappointment and individuals simply are too scared to face that type of pain and fear again and again. In such relationships couples are on a downward spiral, and building a trusting relationship becomes a herculean task.

> Ingrid and Bert were married for twenty years and had four children. Throughout their marriage, Bert

had a number of short-term affairs. Every time he was found out he would promise his wife that he would never do such a thing again. He had a barrel of excuses for why it happened. He would explain that the women "threw themselves on him." Ingrid had no way out of the marriage as she had no qualifications for a job and, with four children, she was "stuck" with Bert. After ten years of misery and mistrust in the relationship, Ingrid went back to school, got herself a job, and separated from her husband. Bert never remarried, but he could not convince Ingrid to go back to him, although he claimed he would never hurt her again and she was the "only love of his life." Without a foundation of trust, love cannot be sustained.

For many people a trusting relationship remains elusive. This happens for a number of reasons. For some people trust is difficult because of past experiences with parents or former partners who have left them with doubts, because of which they are unable to relinquish suspicions about an intimate partner completely.

Tracy grew up in a family where there was a great deal of strife between her parents. Her mother began to confide in 8-year-old Tracy about her father's affair with an office secretary who became pregnant and subsequently had an abortion. Her mother constantly lamented to Tracy that her father had made the secretary pregnant. Her mother would also make statements such as "Men are not be trusted" and "They would easily cheat on a woman." Tracy grew up with this mistrust of men. When she dated, her relationships with men lasted no longer than three months, as Tracy would become obsessively clingy and kept track of everything the boyfriend did and everywhere he went. The man would be impatient and quickly loss interest in her. Tracy had absolutely no trust in men as a result of her parenting and childrearing.

Karen came from a home in which there was no intimacy and developed a negative and distrustful attitude toward all men. She said in therapy, "Men are dogs," and she did not mind playing their game, which was being sexually available and exploiting the men. She was sexually abused by her minister when she was 7 years old and was asked never to talk about it. Later, her father, in a drunken stupor that he claimed he did not remember, sexually abused her. She got back at her father by verbally attacking him, and became the target of her father's violent, angry outbursts. She was also painfully aware of her mother's lack of support. She was the youngest of seven children. Often such people begin to view the sexual act as defining intimacy, and it is difficult for them to separate the two. Frequently, such people say, "If I make someone feel good, then perhaps I can be loved," a haunting and confusing dynamic they carry in their heads.

Some couples start out with high levels of what seems like mutual trust, but they may run out of convincing charitable explanations for the partner's negative behaviors. Such people slowly become worn down from the growing accumulation of negative evidence, and they increasingly entertain doubts about their partner's caring motives.

Belinda was a Realtor who sold homes in an upper-class area. At first her husband, Craig, was thrilled with her accomplishments, although he was not excited about her working with handsome men. One day he went to pay her a surprise visit at the office so they could have dinner together. He walked into her office and realized something was radically wrong. Belinda claimed that a large number of Realtors worked until late in the evening. Craig found Belinda and a handsome man sitting in her office with their arms around each other. Craig was furious—he had kept looking for signs of unfaithfulness. He was very aware of such women; his mother had been one of them. His trust was betrayed and it was doubly difficult to restore it, although Belinda continued to say that nothing happened. With a downward spiral of trust, intimacy gets affected as well.

Sex without love causes pain, said Suing Chin. She was married to Roy, a former army officer who had wanted a Vietnamese wife after he returned from Vietnam. He had met a poor family in Vietnam and they were willing to accept money to send their daughter to Roy as a mail-order bride. Suing Chin was not excited. She would have preferred to marry a Vietnamese, but, being young and inexperienced, she was thrilled about her exposure to a new and different culture. She was 17 and her American husband was over 50. Suing Chin's first response to her husband was fear. She was brought up in a strict, religious, Catholic home and was willing to give her American marriage a new try. Her new husband had sex with her as soon as she arrived at the New York airport. In therapy ten years later, Suing Chin, now a mother of three children, with good knowledge of the English language, said "At 27

> my life is over. I hate sex and I don't mind if my husband has affairs, as long as he leaves me alone. He is a bad man. He has hurt me by always saying I am a throwaway. He doesn't know it, but I think he is a throwaway, too. All he wants is sex and he'll get it anywhere he wants. I don't trust him at all. He always threatens that he'll send me back home and I wish he would. He has girlfriends but now he gets ill and I have to take care of him. I don't like or trust him." Not all Vietnamese marriages with Americans are the same, but this woman had experienced a great deal of pain and fear in her relationship with her husband, with the "rules of relationship," as she saw it, being constantly overlooked.

We develop our sexual attitudes from our parents, schools, peers, and the media, but the most intense influence comes from the family of origin. Trust can be developed at different levels. If there are sexual problems between a couple they are usually accompanied by emotional problems.

> When Rita was ill in bed for two months due to a severe fall that caused painful backaches, Allen was understanding for a few days, but by the second week he was criticizing her and her habits. Before the end of the second month he was critical of her looks and her body. When Rita was ready to have sex, she found out that Allen had had an affair, and she was devastated. This led to angry, bitter fights between them, and, soon, to a great deal of emotional distancing and aloofness, which profoundly affected the children. It is difficult for children to separate emotional and personal problems of parents. If the father is angry with his wife because she

is not willing to have sex with him, he may be irritable and perhaps get into fights with her. What the children observe is emotional pain and distancing, and this has an effect on how children feel about relationships between couples. Silently intertwined with it is the question of sex.

Parents are crucial to our upbringing and have an influence on our personalities and our attitudes toward sex. Although we often hear that we need to learn about sex at home and may believe we do not, in reality we do. When sex is a forbidden topic, when parents talk about it in whispers and it is a "silent, topic," it becomes shrouded with mystery and sometimes negativity. "It is a bad thing to talk about your body parts" is a common comment in such homes. It has an effect on children. When these children grow up, trust with reference to sex and intimacy could become a problem. Trust enables people to develop relationships. Trust between two people enables them to be emotionally vulnerable, to stay open, and to communicate their feelings verbally and combine them with a meaningful sexual relationship. When people block their emotions in the nonsexual aspects of their relationships, their sexual involvements may also be affected or blocked.

Commitment in a relationship comes when a sense of trust exists; paradoxically, for trust to develop, a sense of commitment is required from both partners. One person's constant question about whether he or she should be in a relationship greatly affects the partner's ability to trust and be emotionally and physically vulnerable. In trusting relationships there is an atmosphere of acceptance between partners and an absence of judgment (Beavers 1985).

STRESS FACTORS AND THE LACK OF EMOTIONAL FULFILLMENT

Intimacy in relationships is also affected by stress factors. The stress process includes social factors that influence exposure to strenuous conditions and events, that affect individual and group resources and shape responses to stress. For this purpose, causative factors are labeled *stressors* and responses or effects are labeled *stress outcomes* (Pearlin 1989).

Family stress includes stressors from social organizations, from unemployment, and from extended separations from family members and partners. Changes or life transitions are built into the expectable sequences of family life as children are born, begin school, become adolescents, leave home, and establish their own residences. These are called *normative* stressors, and how family members cope with and adapt to them depends on their relationship and communication abilities.

Families are affected by three major factors that cause stress: (1) a stressor, (2) family resources, and (3) appraisal or interpretation of stressors by the family. How family members or partners deal with stressors depends upon individual and family capacities, resources, and coping effects. A study done by Pearlin and his colleagues (1981) showed the effects of occupational disruptions on emotional distress. One of the biggest stressors in families is unemployment and inadequate income.

Economic changes and the changes in family formation and stability are linked. Marriages stressed by economic uncertainties are more likely to become disrupted. When there is no money to put food on the table, intimacy and togetherness are affected, if this is prolonged, the strains on the relationship becomes burdensome. Menaghan (1995) indicates that as financial pressures rise, husbands and wives treat each other more negatively. They quarrel more and feel increasingly distant. Thoughts of divorce become common and couples struggle to survive. When the economic situation does not become better there is heightened anxiety about job security and an increase in overtime work. The latter in turn causes poor childcare arrangements, which also affects the working abilities of the parents as they constantly worry about their children. Parent–child relations suffer as parents are caught between their jobs and housework. At times, parents become more preoccupied by encroaching problems they face at work and are less responsive to children. At times, marriages end because of money problems and these trends have a number of implications. Women with children may have enduring links, whereas men who divorce and are unemployed *may* lose touch with their biological children but may take on stepfathering responsibilities with other men's children. Children who live with their own divorced biological mother face the additional jeopardy of less money, with the mother's earning capacity not often equaling the father's.

Lack of money can affect every family member's emotional well-being. In intact families the father or mother or both are often depressed, and the emotional support they are able to give or receive is minimal as they focus on the rent that must be paid and the children who must be fed and clothed. The couple may develop distressing patterns of communication, such as withdrawal, or becoming aggressive or argumentative. These patterns of interaction constitute an additional stressor that further affects the family's emotional equilibrium. Because family members are unable to discern the social and economic roots of problematic interaction, they become bewildered by interpersonal difficulties and attribute problems to personality flaws or moral failings. Economic and occupational stressors also affect adults' emotional well-being and parent–child interactions, and they forge an important link in the intergenerational transmission of emotional disadvantages (Menaghan 1995).

Stress has a direct effect on relationships and feelings, particularly when the wife and mother becomes the chief wage earner because the husband is unable to find a job. When one person is overwhelmed with responsibilities and the partner is unemployed, discussions constantly circle around money and responsibilities. Although we talk about equality between sexes, the hard reality in life is that most men do not feel adequate unless they are employed and providing for the family. Ours is a paternalistic society and both men and women still grow up with the expectation that the man will be the primary provider. A married man may be out of work for short periods of time, but total dependency upon his wife, particularly when there are children, is frowned on as irresponsible. The pressure on the man to be the wage earner is intense. Sooner or later, when money is in short supply, the family relationship suffers in terms of unpaid bills, unwanted phone calls, and threats of court procedures. Two people under this pressure cannot be happy with each other. Disruptions happen quickly as family life is affected, and respect for each other as partners diminishes as quarrels about employment and finances overwhelm them.

> Ivan, the father of four children, lost a high-paying job as a construction worker when his company declared bankruptcy. Luckily for him, his wife, Stacy, was very supportive and shared his feeling

that he was unjustly treated because he got very little notice and no severance or vacation pay. The first months passed uneventfully. Ivan was running from place to place looking for something to do. Meanwhile, his wife, an experienced office worker, decided to take a job, although the youngest child was less than 2 years old. She dropped off her daughter with a friend who volunteered to take care of the child for a minimal amount of money. Six months passed and Ivan was still unable to find a job. Stacy was becoming increasingly impatient. The children needed her at home and Ivan was doing less and less housework to help out. In fact, after the first three months, he lay in bed until late in the morning and also spent hours in front of the TV. Overworked, Stacy started to fight him and ridicule him for not finding a job. Their sex life was affected, and the warmth and joviality in the family was fast disappearing. As time passed, Stacy would tease and taunt him in front of the children, without communicating to him her own frustrations about various problems in their lives. The accumulation of bills did not make matters better. Ivan acted as if he did not care, but he was embarrassed, angry, and ashamed of being dependent upon his wife. He became more depressed and less effective in looking for a job. He tried to explain to his angry wife about the number of job applications he had put out and also the number of rejections he received. "Of course, you're incapable of working because you enjoy being my dependent," Stacy said. He wondered about his marriage, as he got no support from her. He also noticed that his children were becoming disrespectful. When his 4-year-old looked up at him and asked, "Daddy, when will you get a job?" Ivan

> flew into a rage and beat his young son black and blue. Stacy was ready to call the police and demanded a divorce. Ivan broke into tears saying that he did not mean to hurt his child. "What is happening to us?" he lamented to his wife. What Ivan and Stacy did not realize was that Ivan was depressed and his self-esteem was at its lowest ebb. By this time communication between husband and wife was at a minimum. They had stopped talking to each other caringly.

It is impossible to talk and be affectionate when an overwhelming accumulation of money problems face a family and their lifestyle is affected. Money is a powerful issue in marriages and should never be overlooked, as it may be the worst stressor and a rapid destroyer of relationships and communications.

Besides the stress that is connected to money, there are many other stresses in a marriage. There is stress in the birth of a child, stress in confronting in-law and child–parent problems. Stress is ever-present in marriage, with children, in-laws, parents, and siblings, at the workplace and at home. There is no life without some stress, and how it is handled becomes critical.

The timing of a given stress may also have a profound effect on a marriage. For example, when a married woman goes back to college to get a graduate degree, her marriage may break up while she is a student. Most likely to divorce are couples with children born before one or both of the parents enter graduate school. Women who give birth to children after graduate school have fewer divorces (Pearlin 1981). To a large extent it depends upon the husband as well. Supportive husbands may tend to neutralize the stress for wives in graduate school, but this does not reduce it for wives who already have children. Often the women are caught in the stress of marital disruption when they try to balance student life and mothering roles. Other factors can include the husband's difficulties in coping with the changes in the wife's roles. In fact, every marriage has its own specific pressures, losses, and stresses. The strain itself often impairs the partners' capacity to deal with these problems.

Under stress, people may suffer from faulty thinking. During this time people are more apt to be irritable and lose their tempers, to have tunnel vision, and to overgeneralize and catastrophize. All of these factors come to the fore when we are under stress. In a family with two wage earners, which is very common, there are also pressures from the outside. When the job is going well there is no pressure and the couple is happy with each other.

> Lydia mentioned, "When I am doing well in my job [as a manager of a boutique] and not under stress, Collins can do no wrong. He is almost perfect." But when things are not going right in the workplace, everything he does is wrong. Collins had promised to fix her computer so that she could finish her work. He needed a particular tool to work with the intricate parts of the computer and promised to work on it, but he forgot to buy it. When Collins got home, Lydia had this conversation, when she was completely stressed out and irritable.
>
> *Collins:* Oh, I forgot it again.
> *Lydia:* What do you mean you forgot it? You already forgot it once. You know I have to complete my assignment for my boutique class. How can you

forget, after I called you on the phone not once but twice?

Collins: I'm sorry. I got very busy and I tend to be absent-minded about these things.

Lydia: You shouldn't have forgotten it!

Collins: The big boss came to the office and had everyone on their toes. He asked to see some of my work and everything else flew out of my head.

Lydia: You care about your boss more than you care about me.

Collins (getting upset): That's not true. You're angry and overreacting.

What happened between Collins and Lydia could happen to anyone. When people are upset they tend to discount reasonable explanations, and cling to negative, personalized interpretations such as "You don't care about me," which does not make the situation better. When people are stressed there is a slip in control over their thinking and behaviors. They find it too difficult to moderate their extreme interpretations, correct their distortions, or regulate how they express their feelings. People under stress can respond by becoming verbally abusive, physically assaultive, or completely withdrawn (Beck 1989). They can also regress in their behaviors, clinging to the partner and becoming totally dependent upon him or her, showing that they need the partner constantly. Stress that appears in different ways, when not dealt with forthrightly, can lead to other serious difficulties, including sexual problems and unfulfillment.

NEGATIVE EMOTIONAL AND SEXUAL FULFILLMENT

Relationships involve being able to share and be comfortable with one's partner. In the beginning stages two people who are getting to know each other are likely to be very attentive to each other's needs. Listening is a skill, a technique that most couples who have been married to each other for some time forget. The ability to listen can create a sense of intimacy. Knowing that someone listens to you and cares about you is a powerful feeling, but as time passes and this skill is not used it may break down, because of outside pressures and because people are not taught how to listen effectively. Another barrier to communication is that, as time goes on in a marriage or long-term relationship, emotions such as anger, hurt, and fear *can* become increasingly intense and negative. As Beavers (1985) indicates, after a commitment has been made, people believe they no longer need to be on their best behavior. Couples may also believe after commitment that it is safer and easier to let out their anger and resentment without fear of abandonment by their partners.

Emotional fulfillment in a relationship is enhanced when the persons involved make a conscious contribution to the commitment. Having children provides a common bond, and having good relationships and making friends with new relatives and in-laws is important. Life does not come with a ready-made plan. People lose jobs, partners may be infertile and not capable of having children, and in-laws may not be affectionate or friendly. Rules change in the family of origin. A talkative wife may discover that a husband is not a good communicator when it comes to discussing his problems. Problems in the workplace cannot be pushed under the rug and must be discussed elsewhere. With poor communication between partners, coldness and distancing begin to play a role in such marriages. When there are problems in a marriage and they are not worked through, they spill over into other relationships, including the relationships with the children. All these factors begin to affect relationships, and, with emotional distancing, sexual desires diminish and the partners communicate less and less.

At some point children may begin to be used as *tools* to carry on the marriage and the family. In marriages in which couples are insecure or have moved away from each other, children can be used to keep the marriage going. Such children carry a degree of ambivalence concerning their parents' marriage. This makes them ideal recruits for the role of go-between, as they want their parents to stay together. One of them, however, may be treated as a favorite child by one of the parents. The child's ambivalence may be reinforced by both parents, who feel some relief at finding that it decreases their own escalating fights and conflicts (Byng-Hall 1989). There is further development of this scenario if a closer relationship begins to develop between mother and son. The mother may criticize the father to the child and the child may feel important in playing the role of "Mama's real friend." Quite often in such situations the child becomes the parent's confidante and the one who carries messages back and forth. Although the child may feel a sense of disloyalty, this is quickly overcome by the importance of the new role that he begins to play. Couples whose bonding is unstable often remain tied together by children who elicit caregiving responses from each parent. A grandson may hold his mother and grandmother together in the same way, and a clinging mother–child dyad can keep all others out (Byng-Hall 1989). Often, parents who have grown up in families where intimacy was superficial and emotional incest was present may seek the same in their own families of procreation. When loneliness in the marriage becomes a serious issue, couples turn elsewhere for companionship and love. Infidelity and affairs outside the marriage may begin.

Parents who are alienated from each other may develop a close relationship with a child of the opposite or same sex; at times they may develop an incestuous sexual relationship with a child or children. Often incest is an intergenerational pattern. This may occur when the marital relationship is overwhelmed by hatred and anger. More commonly, however, people in barren or troubled relationships will also seek emotional and sexual fulfillment elsewhere. If the person values honesty and monogamy, the affair will probably take its toll in guilt and shame. In other cases children are used to satisfy the parents' need for intimacy and power. Many incest victims do not tell about their victimization. They keep quiet; not because they are afraid to tell someone that something happened, not because they are afraid of hurting themselves, but often because they are afraid of breaking up the family or getting their parents in trouble.

> Susan, a 36-year-old woman, typifies the classic loyal child. She was afraid that she would hurt her father and lose his love, which appeared to be more powerful than any desire to get help. "Looking back, I realize that my father had me right where he wanted me. He told me that if I talked to anyone about what we were doing, it would be the end of the family. He said that I had a very important part in all that we did. He added that if I talked, my mother would send him away, and that they'd send me away to a foster home. Everyone in the family would hate me."

Although it is true to some degree that incest does shatter the family, it is in the child's best interests for this to happen, although the breakup may be an emotional burden on the child and the child may feel responsible.

Another type of emotional distancing happens because of in-law problems. Rejection of a daughter-in-law or son-in-law creates problems for the new, beginning family. In such situations extended family members are part of the marital conflict. There are often loyalty alignment triangles in such families. The husband, for example, may be in an overly close relationship with his family of origin, with the wife in the outside position. There is no membership or appropriate type of bonding with the wife. Family of origin has the strongest influence on him.

> Aaron, who was overly attached to his sister, Megan, provided for her and her family because her husband was unemployed. Megan, in turn, took care of his household bills. Eventually, Aaron fell in love and got married. His new marriage made Megan insecure. Aaron, realizing her insecurity, called her while he was on his honeymoon. Megan cried while discussing her family issues, and Aaron was unhappy during his honeymoon. His wife, Sheila, was hurt and ready to pack up and leave, but Aaron assured her that this would never happen again. Sheila, however, found herself in a one-down position in her relationship with him and his hostile family. But with marital therapy they were able to work through their issues and create a life for themselves separate from his family of origin.

> Dale was very attached to his sister Karen, and they ran a company together. Although married, his sister was very dependent upon her brother as her husband was unemployed and did not bother to

look for a job. Their mother encouraged this relationship between brother and sister and also discouraged the son from getting married. The family was happy that Karen had two sons to carry on the family business. Dale was not encouraged to go out with women, but since he was over 30 years old they did not have any control over him. His occasional dates were seen as unimportant nuisances they had to tolerate. Finally Dale met the woman of his dreams and fell in love. None of his family members were happy, however, as they saw her as someone who would usurp Dale's affections; the mother was overly concerned about her daughter, whom she really saw as her son's dependent. They proceeded to downplay his girlfriend. When he married her, however, they began to mistreat her, to make jokes about her, and worked at creating problems between the two. Karen constantly complained about how cunning and money-minded her sister-in-law was; Dale listened to her and found himself in conflict with his wife. Emotional and sexual intimacy suffered.

THE ROLE OF FAMILY SECRETS

Another detriment to happiness and a source of serious problems in the marriage and with the children occurs in a home where there are secrets. Imber-Black (1993) explains secrets as a systemic phenomenon. "They are relational, shaping dyads, triangles, hidden alliances, splits, cut-offs, defining boundaries" (p. 9) of who is "in" and who is "out," and create closeness or distancing in families. Information about who knows the secret and who is kept in the dark orients us to the way in which secrets affect relationships.

Secrets reflect intergenerational loyalties. Certain

behaviors that seem to make no sense may be a way of dealing with events and patterns the family wishes to keep hidden. This might include affairs, serious crimes, addiction, or homosexuality (Imber-Black 1993).

When there are family secrets, family members are required to keep the secret to avoid being viewed as disloyal and subjected to the family's wrath. However, the capacity to keep a secret is undermined when two loyalties collide. For example, when a child has to keep a secret with a parent that excludes the other parent, or when one spouse keeps a secret that directly affects the well-being of his or her partner, then secrecy and loyalty are easily compromised.

A secret is information, information that is owed to another but withheld. Secrets may protect a person by concealing something. Secrets may also be related to cultural taboos around money, sex, physical and mental illnesses, addictions, or AIDS. It has also been found that one person's secret can be another person's victimization and shame.

> Darcie learned that her brother, Dillon, had had an affair with his wife's sister, Anna. Darcie walked into her brother's bedroom assuming that her sister-in-law, Jill, was home alone. She was completely taken aback when she saw her brother naked with Jill's younger sister. Darcie walked out confused and embarrassed. Her brother made her promise that she would not divulge this information to his wife, as he did not wish to lose her or their children. Darcie agreed. It was Darcie's secret but she would hiss about it to her brother whenever they had a misunderstanding or quarrel. She was one-up on him and he felt victimized.

Shame is a very powerful motivator of human progress. It can drive people to achieve perfection, status, and wealth. It is no surprise that 38 percent of American corporate executives grew up in alcoholic families (Mason 1993). Shame also has the effect of creating control in a person. Coleman (1987) notes that in order to move away from the pain of shame, which is the "master emotion," people are often driven to addictive behaviors that give moments of release by making a person feel better or numb. A compulsive executive, for example, did not want her husband to know her painful secret. After he found out, they went into therapy, but it took them almost a year before she could reveal what she saw as a greater source of shame: her incestuous relationship with her alcoholic father.

Secrets almost always inhibit growth. However, it is not the secret itself, as painful or embarrasing as it may feel at the time, that creates lasting psychological problems. It is the family process around the event or experience that is the major determinant of how it affects the persons involved. If a family is relatively open, its members are free to comment on what happened and it can also be passed on through family stories. In such circumstances the family is less likely to be bound by shame. Families who are closed and loyal to their secrets develop rules of "Don't talk, don't trust, don't feel," and create family myths and dishonest stories to hide their secrets. This kind of emotional climate becomes the source of internalized conflicts and disturbed relationships within and outside the family.

As Fossum and Mason (1986, pp. 86–87) indicate, there are eight rules that govern how a family deals with secrets.

1. They are in control of all behavior and interactions.

2. They emphasize being perfect, that is, always doing the "right thing" and always being right.

3. Blaming is another aspect of shame. If something did not happen in the manner in which it was planned, then somebody has to be blamed. This can be someone else or oneself.

4. Denial is important for maintaining shame, denying negative or vulnerable feelings like anxiety, fear, grief, or rejection.

5. People who are ashamed do not expect reliability or constancy in relationships. They are always looking out for the unpredictable.

6. They believe in incompleteness, that is, they do not bring transactions to completion because they might have to face feelings or honest revelations that they are protecting.

7. There is the rule of "Don't talk," that is, do not talk openly about shameful, abusive, or compulsive behaviors.

8. When there is disrespectful, shameful, abusive, or compulsive behavior, disqualify it, deny it, or disguise it.

Following these rules not only instills shame but perpetuates it. The process in the family is powerfully galvanized against the expression of any honest feelings or open disclosures. Family members tend to learn these rules unconsciously and learn not to ask and not to comment. In this manner information owed to the family becomes a shameful secret. These rules become the cause and the result of the secret (Imber-Black 1993). These rules organize a family's dynamics, and the family becomes shame-bound as children learn to absorb unexpressed feelings and stories.

Fossum and Mason (1986) indicate that a shame-bound family is a family with a self-sustaining, multigenerational system of interaction with a cast of characters who are (or were in their lifetime) loyal to a set of rules and injunctions demanding control, perfectionism, blame, and denial. The pattern inhibits or defeats the development of authentic, intimate relationships, and promotes secrets and vague personal boundaries. This process unconsciously instills shame in family members as well as chaos in their lives, and binds them to perpetuate the shame in themselves and their kin. It does so regardless of the good intentions, wishes, and love that may also be part of the system. When family members maintain the shame and do not discuss the issues, shame is maintained as part of an interpersonal process that is learned in families. One's childhood sense of family is built from limited tools and incomplete data. Children see themselves as the center of the universe and absorb events personally. The child, like a computer, codes and stores every experience and event. Childhood perceptions are the birthplace of our processing abilities, that is, how we learn to be in the world, to see ourselves, and to be in relationships. Imber-Black (1993) specifies that these perceptions can be images that we project onto the screen of the mind; they shape our interpretations of our life experiences and the meanings we take with us as we live as adults. Children tend to view the behavior patterns they live with as normal, no matter how deviant they might be in wider society. Family therapist Schwartz (1985) states: "As long as we are content to stay within the confines of the memories, recollections and conclusions about our family formed out of our childhood experiences, we are destined to continue to enact our childhood position of no-choice reactor to the forces—conscious and unconscious—in our familes" (p. 1).

Closely related to secrets are lies, which serve to protect the secrets. As Imber-Black (1993) reveals, many secrets in people's lives have to do not so much with tragedies but with the problems caused by lies or denial. With secrets also come guilt and injustice. Secrets, shame, and guilt lead to loss of intimacy. How can one be intimate when the ingredients of love and trust are missing?

In his play *The Iceman Cometh,* Eugene O'Neill discusses an injustice a man did to his wife. He talks to his friends about it. "And Evelyn always knew about the tarts I'd been with when I came from a trip. She'd kiss me and look in the eyes, and she'd know. . . . God, can you picture all I made her suffer, and all the guilt she made me feel, and how I hated myself. If only she hadn't been so damned good—she'd been the same kind of wife I was a husband."

Infidelity is one of the most devastating problems in marriages, and it affects and is affected by intimacy. With infidelity comes another ugly problem of imbalances. How do you repair a marriage that has been imbalanced by lies, deceit, and guilt? How do you make the partners re-create a more or less meaningful and symmetrical relationship without discussing the problem of infidelity? How do you help re-create trust, which is the basis of all true relationships, when it has been lost in a destructive marriage?

> Mindy and Mylan came for therapy as a last resort to rework their marriage. They had been married for fifteen years and separated for two years. Before they got a divorce they wanted to give their marriage a "last try" because they had two children and Mylan

> felt "in spite of everything" they were made for each other. Their problem was that Mylan had had an affair and Mindy found out. In therapy Mylan had revealed that he had over fifteen affairs. He explained to his wife that they were not affairs but "flings." She was horrified and wanted a divorce. Mylan, with belated insight, sadly commented, "So much of everything I had, my home, children, and wife, for so little." In spite of therapy, this marriage did not work; the secrets, lies, unfaithfulness, and disloyalty took their toll.

In therapeutic work there is usually no possibility of developing a meaningful relationship that has been skewed by the dance of guilt, injustice, and presumed innocence as long as the couple is unwilling to discuss the secrets and lies, because during this time not all the sources of power are disclosed and balanced. The hidden weapons of innocence can be as strong as those of permanent betrayal. The anger of the innocent party and the guilt of the unfaithful have to be disclosed and worked through for any amount of trust to be re-created.

Another form of secret occurs between parents and children. If a parent and a child share an unhealthy secret about the other parent, then they form a negative alliance. Secrets can create hidden alliances and coalitions in families. For example, the mother who promises not to tell her husband that their unmarried teenage daughter has had an abortion creates a negative alliance between herself and her daughter. Secrets also become political weapons that children and parents can use against each other. They can create and use boundaries to manipulate relationships. Siblings with secrets can use them to blackmail each other. One may say to the other, "I'll tell about your stealing the money if you don't do what I tell you to!" A mother can tell her son, "I'll tell your father about your smoking if you don't behave."

In secrets, normally one person is held hostage until the secret is exposed, and then the secret loses its power. All these factors take precedence when family members cannot talk to each other, when they cannot follow the rules that have to be flexible in the family, and when there is no intimacy. With intimacy and trust in family relationships there is no need to hide matters because everything can be discussed openly and honestly.

There are other types of secrets that create serious problems in family relationships, and if help is not offered in a timely fashion they can destroy individuals and families.

INCEST IN THE FAMILY

Why do parents turn to their children for a sexual relationship? Besides breaking the most basic taboo in our culture, incest reflects on the spatial relationship and the lack of intimacy in a marriage. Obviously, not all parents who are unfulfilled in their marriages have sex with their children. They turn to outside relationships, alcohol, or drugs, or merely wither away in silence and pain.

Incest, a common form of child abuse, can be described as any sexual contact between a child or adolescent and a person who is closely related or perceived to be related, including stepparents and live-in partners.

It is a serious crime against a child, and different from other forms of sexual abuse in that the perpetrator is assumed to stand in a protective, parental role to the victim. That person, a parent or an adult who is supposed to offer comfort and understanding, violates the trust by sexualizing the relationship. Between a child and an adult there can be no true consent, equality, trust, or safety because of the overwhelming power imbalance.

In incest, tension, fear, betrayal, pain, and mistrust color the victim's sexual awakening. In these situations children are robbed of the opportunity to experience sex as something that is primarily for themselves. Quite often, survivors blame themselves for not stopping the abuse. Other children, who have distant and punitive mothers or receive affection only from the father, may after the incestuous initiation participate willingly in order to get attention from an older adult. Many children lack the maturity to identify what was wrong and are thus incapable of expressing it. The perpetrator's emotional needs and selfish orientation toward sexuality dominate the child.

The legal definition of incest is extremely narrow, and defines incest as sexual intercourse between relatives. Many young people do not realize they have been violated because they have not been penetrated by the adult. From a psychological perspective, however, incest covers a wide range of behaviors and relationships. They include physical contact with a child's mouth, breasts, genitals, anus, or any other part of the body with the explicit purpose of sexually arousing the aggressor. Other types of incest involve no physical contact with the child's body, but include masturbation of the aggressor in front of the child, or having the child pose for sexually suggestive photographs. Kissing and hugging children is necessary for their own as well as the parents' emotional well-being, but if the touching or kissing is sexually suggestive or stimulating it is clearly incestuous. The fact that the perpetrator insists on secrecy is the tacit admission that this is so.

A number of other behaviors are called *psychological*

incest. Victims of this type of incest may not have actually been touched, but their privacy or safety has been violated. Invasive acts include spying on a child who is bathing or dressing, or making explicit, suggestive, seductive, or sexually explicit comments to a child. Although this may not appear to be incest, the victims often feel violated and suffer many of the same psychological symptoms as actual incest victims.

From the outside, many incest families look like any other family, but on the inside the families are riddled with secrets and psychological stress.

> Anita, a beautiful olive-skinned woman in her twenties, talked about incest with her stepfather.
>
> "He was a giant of a man in our community. My stepfather was a well-known businessman and respected minister in a church that had a real big congregation. He was a pillar of our community. In church he would preach about moral sins and how sinners should be punished and everybody loved him. But I knew him better. Often I wanted to scream and call him a liar and a hypocrite because he had destroyed my virginity when I was 13 years old. He screwed me so many times that I wondered how he could go to church and act like a man of God." Anita came from an outwardly model family.

> Lisa faced a different form of abuse. Her father would grab her from behind and pinch her breasts and laugh about it. He would pay her to undress before him. He would beg her to touch his penis and repaid her with gifts. Lisa was scared and embarrassed. Outwardly, she too came from a model family.
>
> Lisa mentioned in therapy that in her family they

> never talked about how they felt. If something bothered her, she would just push it down. Her mother had been fairly affectionate to her as a child. She would hug and kiss her. This died out when she was 4 years old. Lisa never saw any affection between her mother and her father. They always did things together as a family—outings every Sunday, dinner in expensive restaurants every Saturday night, and movies once a week at least—but there was never any real closeness. Her father was apparently lonely and needed intimacy. Sometimes he would ask Lisa to French-kiss him; at times she was afraid not to do it as he would look at her so intensely; at other times she would refuse, at which point he would beg her and say he just needed to be close to her.

Adults who are offenders suffer from psychological distress, emotional isolation, and emotional immaturity. Their thoughts about sexuality are distorted, as they have not experienced intimate relationships with anyone and have poor impulse control. Perpetrators are also brought up by punitive and distant parents, and may be victims of incest themselves. Abusive people feel inadequate and powerless. They suffer from low self-esteem and do not have happy marriages. They also feel chronically resentful toward others and develop a sense of power in the families of procreation. They are self-appointed experts in all family matters. They know everything, from childbirth to the political future of the country. They tend to involve themselves in the minute details of each family member's life.

They use their power as the adult and parent to isolate other family members from the outside world. They may deliberately embarrass visitors or directly forbid family members to interact with others. They are dictatorial in private, but in public seem kind and understanding. Information about the actual behaviors in the family would always shock outsiders. The perpetrators learn to mask it well.

Perpetrators have tremendous feelings of isolation. They use drugs, alcohol, and other forms of escape to sidestep the pain they feel inside. Their escape into drugs impairs their functioning by lowering their inhibitions. Their own needs are so overwhelming and overpowering that they ignore or deny the pain they are causing their victims. Distorted thinking encourages an offender to victimize a child who depends upon him.

The adult offender often rationalizes that he is being seduced by the child. As one man commented about his 9-year-old daughter, with whom he had a sexual relationship, "She would swing her hips and shake herself and walk in front of me, and she liked me to button up her dresses!"

Another man commented that he wanted his child to learn about sex "properly." He said to the probation officer, "I love my daughter and I wanted to be the first person to teach her how to do it. My love for her is pure and I *had* to show and teach her all about sex." Another offender defensively said that he was not the only one having pleasure—his daughter did too: "She felt good and also very special." Sometimes they make statements such as, "I am not going outside the family to satisfy my needs; it is all *within* the family."

There is a great deal of distorted thinking in sexual abuse, coupled with the imposition of inappropriate arousal patterns in the child. When incest begins, it takes on an addictive pattern. As one victim recalled as an adult, "I hated it when he started coming into my room and talking in a soft, seductive voice. . . . I hate all men who talk like that."

Not all incest victims are girls. Men and boys are also victims, having been sexually abused by their mother, father, or significant other. Incest in boys or adolescents also leads to adult problems.

> Julius, a 40-year-old man, complained in therapy about a wide range of sexual difficulties he had in relationships with women, including recurrent impotence. Talking to him about his sexual history revealed that he was sexually abused by his mother from the time he was 8 until he was 15 or 16.
>
> Julius said that his mother would call him the "love of her life." She would fondle him and make him fondle her and finally have oral sex with him. She continued to call him the love of her life. It affected Julius to such an extent that when he dated women he felt guilty and disloyal to his mother, although he knew that this was irrational. At the time I saw him, he was in a long-term relationship, but had developed a number of sexual problems including impotence.
>
> The affectionate and seductive manner in which his mother molested him bound him to her in many ways. He was angry, guilty, a victim, but a part of him was protecting her and her love for him. With a father who abandoned him when he was 4, he had no male role models but only a deeply depressed, psychotic mother.

Incestuous relationships between mother and son are not common. When present, the mother is usually mentally ill or close to it.

Boys or young male adolescents can also be abused by their fathers or other adult male relatives, but there is a particular problem faced *only* by men. It arises from the fact that our culture provides no room for a man to act as victim. Men are not supposed to be victims. A "real man" is expected to be able to protect himself in any situation. He is supposed to solve every problem one way or another. When a man experiences victimization our culture expects him to deal with it like a man, which often translates into avenging hurt and then forgetting about it. If a man is not able to do that, or is unwilling to resort to this type of behavior, he is seen as a coward and unmanly. Although there is no logic to this type of thinking, it is a rare individual who has not unconsciously internalized these attitudes to some degree. A male survivor of abuse may understand that violent revenge would be a dangerous response to his situation, but can still feel like a weakling for not resorting to violence. Men are supposed to be in control of their feelings at all times. The survivor's ongoing feelings of confusion, frustration, anger, and fear can become further evidence of his failings as a man. Since men are not supposed to be victims, they aren't men. Usually the victimized male begins to worry about what the abuse has turned him into. He sees himself as being an inadequate male; he may also see himself as a child, a woman, as gay, or less than human—an irreparably damaged freak (Lew 1988).

> When Clinton was 6 years old, his stepfather violently abused him and then forced him into oral sex. Clinton was scared and started to cry. His behavior was considered to be weak and brought forth an even more violent response from his stepfather. As Lew (1988) indicates, this behavior is considered

> weak and unmasculine and becomes a justification for the adult's brutality. Clinton mentioned to his therapist that he had to learn to control his tears and fears to avoid triggering renewed physical or sexual attacks. His stepfather told him many times, "Stand up and stop cringing. You look like a defeated dog." Then, Clinton continued, "He would abuse me again," often using the phrase, "Stop crying or I'll give you something more to cry about." The message Clinton got was to keep his feelings in check or else. Thus he learned to hide, deny, and control his emotions. When he spoke about the pain there was no expression of the emotions he talked about. By the time he had reached adulthood he had mastered the technique very well.

Lew (1988) says, "Learning to thaw this emotional ice jam is a difficult process, but one that is essential to recover" (p. 241). Feelings are a source of great confusion to the male incest survivor. He is afraid of having them—and afraid of not having them.

Multigenerational abuse is also common in some families. It is destructive, but it becomes a part of their lives and "the beat goes on." In such situations, until they understand and work it through, abused children may choose partners who are abused as well; this is an unconscious process. In intergenerational abuse it is difficult to blame anyone or view one as a victim and another as the abuser.

> In a difficult case, two sons, Wilbur and Vincent, aged 14 and 15, were alternately sexually abused by their mother, Miriam. They were placed in a residential setting and saw one another as rivals for their mother's love; consequently, they hated each

other. Once they tried to hurt each other physically when the mother was overtly affectionate to one son in front of the other. In therapy, the mother was very talkative, as well as very infantile. She talked about herself, her sons, and her father, who had sexually abused her. She was afraid to have both sons together with her in therapy. She mentioned that it was almost like having too many grownups in one room and she could not handle it.

Miriam was the one chosen by her father. She commented about sexually abusing her sons that she was doing them a favor, just as her father had done for her. She had been "introduced to sex" by her father and he had promised to teach her everything. Her sister had also been abused by the father although, she added in an infantile manner, Miriam was his "favorite." He told her that "she could do it better than anyone else." She therefore questioned what was wrong with her introducing her sons to sex. How do you deal with such a client? Is she the victim or the abuser? Obviously, both.

The chronic transactional pattern prevalent in this family had existed for a long time; with it arose many dysfunctional structures. In talking with Miriam's mother, Jo Anne, who had become Miriam's dependent, it was clear that she had made Miriam feel guilty by accusing her of "stealing" her husband away from her. She saw Miriam more as a rival than a daughter, and a distorted parent—child relationship developed. Miriam became the parent and caretaker of her mother, who was just as infantile as Miriam. While talking about Miriam's father, Jo Anne mentioned that he was his mother's favorite child and smiled knowingly. Was there another generation of abuse? It's hard to tell but easy to assume (Pillari 1991).

In such families intimacy between married couples is absent, and children are viewed as property to be used and misused as dictated by their own upbringing and the flaws that were part of it.

CHAPTER FOUR

Family Dynamics and the Effects on Child Development

A MARRIED COUPLE IN THERAPY complained of a problem that I have encountered time and again in my practice. Patrick, age 40, and Carmen, 38, had had divorce papers drawn up because their marriage appeared to be stalemated. However, before the legalities were finalized, they wanted to try one more time to salvage their marriage. Carmen complained, "I know we love each other, but there's no intimacy in our marriage. I'm living in a house of strangers. We never sit down for dinner together. We do our own thing. I don't know what he's feeling."

Lack of intimacy has different dynamics in different case situations. For instance, in some families there is a subcultural ideology that involves a *desperate preoccupation*. As one mother insisted, with the father echoing her thoughts, "We are a happy family. Our son is a normal, happy child, and you couldn't find anyone happier. I'm pleased with my son and my husband. I'm pleased with life. I have been happily married for twenty years and we haven't had a single quarrel or misunderstanding. We've had twenty years of the happiest married life you could ever imagine." This statement came from a mother and father whose teenage son was referred to therapy because he was playing hookey from school and was involved in drugs. The dynamics of this family indicate bland, determined approval of each person's interests and activities with no consideration of whether they are actually compatible with the family's (or society's) code of values. If the family members were so well balanced and happy with each other and stable in their relationships, why was the young adolescent referred to therapy? The family myth maintained that "everything is fine," and problems were ignored until the boy got into trouble in school.

Apparently, in the second case as in the first, there is poor communication. Communication patterns derive from the family culture, the degree of emotional fusion or distance, and the types of invisible loyalties maintained by the family members. When there is no real intimacy present between family members, there is the phenomenon of pseudomutuality.

As Wynne and colleagues (1958) described, "There is a part of every person that is striving for relatedness to other human beings" (p. 206), and there is another part which is simultaneously striving to develop a sense of personal identity. To resolve this dilemma, two types of solutions may evolve. There is *genuine mutuality* in families whose members care about each other and wish to connect with each other in real and caring ways, and there is *pseudomutuality* when key family members have "a predominant absorption in fitting together at the expense of the differentiation of the identities of the persons" (Wynne et al. 1958, p. 207).

Families who have mutual relationships are less

likely to have serious problems in a marriage because they have the capability to tolerate differences of opinions and at the same time respect each other for their differences. Mutuality deals with the process of continuing relational renewal and reengagement. In mutuality there is a shared commitment to reshape the relationship as the life cycle unfolds, as new and unexpected events take place, as new interests and aspirations emerge. Mutuality optimizes the likelihood of intimacy. There are families who come to therapy because they are in a transitional situation in their lives. Divergence, conflict, and changes due to growth and maturity emerge, and these may generate many outcomes for relational systems other than mutuality.

> Kelly and Genet were married, but spent all their vacations and free time with their own separate friends, until it came to a point when they did not miss or care about each other. It appeared to Genet that they were merely sharing a home and a bed. When she brought this up, her husband was resentful, and blamed her for the coolness that took over their marriage. Before long it was clear that Kelly as well as Genet wanted out; with no desire to work on the marriage, they got a divorce.

Without desire for reengagement, and without help, such relationships may be discarded with no possible exploration of reengagement at a different level. In such cases, the couple may lack problem-solving skills and the ability to plan for the household and work through tasks together. When problems overwhelm the skills and resources of the couple, the relationship becomes lost in a sea of unmet needs and alienation.

Enduring relatedness requires periodic stock-taking,

with each person taking into account his or her own needs and preferences, those of the other, and the quality of what goes on between them. The result of such stock-taking may alter the previous relationship.

In other situations the relationship may take on "pathological" forms such as pseudomutuality or pseudohostility (Wynne 1961). In such situations the family preserves a fixed pattern of relatedness that takes priority at the expense of individual needs and despite changing circumstances. In his classic study Wynne specifies that in pseudo mutuality, the subjective tension aroused by divergence or independence of expectations, including open affirmation of a sense of personal identity, is experienced as not merely disrupting that particular transaction, but as possibly demolishing the entire relationship with abandonment, death, or psychosis (Wynne et al. 1958). In other circumstances, change is not negotiated but simply asserted by one person, seemingly at the expense of others.

> Frederick was the older of two children by five years. The mother doted on Frederick until Dwayne was born. Dwayne was puny and thin, unlike Frederick, who was tall, big-boned, and strong. The mother visualized her family as "happy."
>
> In conversations with her sons she told them she wanted to divide everything equally. They went on many outings, and did a lot together as a family. As Frederick grew, he was told that he had to manage the family business. Thus, at age 22, Frederick was the head of a manufacturing company. Although Dwayne lived away from home with his wife, the mother constantly called him, asking him to be an actual partner to the brother in the business. At the same time, other rules were laid down, including one stipulating that only Frederick, not Dwayne,

should be allowed to negotiate deals. Frederick had to travel to meet people and work on site so that all the work could be supervised and completed. His younger brother took money from the office and squandered it, but the parents insisted that both sons get the same paycheck. Frederick objected, saying he was the director and could not pay his brother the same amount, but the fact that he ran the company made no difference to his family. Thus Frederick had to share everything he made, including his personal investments, with his playful, pleasure-loving brother. Although Dwayne often took long vacations, the mother insisted to outsiders that they did the same amount of work. Any successes that Frederick had were always mentioned as being achieved by both children. When Frederick complained that it was impossible for him to run everything by himself and that his brother was not an equal partner because of all the restrictions the family had placed on him in terms of work responsibilities, the mother denied it, saying, "You do equal amounts of work." If the father defended Frederick, the mother would flare up and ask her husband, "Whose side are you on? I'm the one who feeds you and you can't do anything without me." This statement silenced the father, and the mother, in total denial of Frederick's pain, would continue to declare that the sons put in equal amounts of work. When Frederick wanted to marry a girl who lived near them, the mother insisted she was not good enough. To Frederick she said repeatedly, "I will celebrate a funeral if you bring her home." Thus the mother totally controlled the family situation, and had a pseudomutual relationship with her husband and her sons in which there were no opportunities for any opinion except the domineering mother's, and consequently everything went her way.

As Forward (1989) indicates, parents who focus their energies on their own physical and emotional survival send out a powerful message to their children: "Your feelings are not important. I'm the only one that counts." When such family dynamics exist, the children in such homes do not develop a sense of self-worth, because their parents do not validate their needs and feelings. Usually the parents' needs are so overwhelming that they can feel only for themselves.

When Samantha's mother cried, Samantha shared her mother's pain and cried with her. However, the mother did not seem to care about Samantha's feelings. When Samantha reached her late twenties she felt something was wrong with her and went to a therapist. When she mentioned this to her mother, the mother showed no interest and pretended she had not heard. The toxic message from her mother, as well as her father, came out loud and clear—she was a nonentity to them. What really counted was their feelings and not hers. Samantha felt good only when she made her parents feel good; if she made them feel bad, then she was bad.

When Samantha moved out of her parents' home, she felt considerable anxiety about defining her identity. She was anxious, scared, and confused while on her own, because her independent thoughts, feelings, and needs had never been encouraged. She did not know what to expect in a genuine loving relationship. In therapy Samantha was angry because she finally understood that she had been used by her parents, and was ready to confront her

> feelings of emotional abandonment. In a slow but steady manner Samantha began to set limits on what she would give of herself to others and also to respect her own rights, needs, and feelings. By looking out for herself she was becoming a person who was real, worthy, and visible to others.

The manner in which a family deals with its different members also lays the groundwork for intimacy and the beginnings of sexuality.

> Emily, a woman in her late seventies living in a nursing home, told me that from a very young age she had taught her daughters that sex was bad and that sex was all men were interested in. Emily grew up with the family myth, "Men are bad people interested only in exploiting women for sexual purposes." This perception set up a tug of war in this family, with the women aligned against the men. Emily's two daughters were also trained to think of men as bad. Emily's mother began this intergenerational pattern with her two daughters by constantly putting her husband down as she described him as being interested only in sex. Both daughters identified with her.

Children identify with their parents in a two-step process. As the process begins, children of both sexes usually make an initial identification with their mother; boys later change their identification to their father while girls maintain the mother as a primary model.

A family and its structure has an effect on how sex-role patterns are developed. Beside identification with a parent, the original biological differences are overlaid by many response systems that are sustained according to their appropriateness with other family members, peers, teachers, and the opposite sex. In Emily's family the sex roles that members played would unfold in the following manner.

Emily claimed that the women were viewed only as sex objects by their men and men were viewed as the aggressors by the women. Women in this family responded to the men's needs, but they maintained adamantly that they did not enjoy sex. While Emily stated in no uncertain terms that sex was a taboo topic in the family, whenever an occasion arose, she would graphically describe how one person, a family member or a neighbor, behaved sexually. Though the implicit family rule and myth appeared to say "Do not discuss sex in the family," there appeared to be a preoccupation with the subject. Another fascinating phenomenon in this family was the fact that women would cling to each other in all matters, while there was no emotional intimacy between the women and the men. However, when choosing a mate, they would suddenly become aggressively independent. Their choice of mate might be poor, but they would stay with it and not take any advice. They became self-righteous in denying their need to marry weak or alcoholic men. These marriages also fulfilled the protective and defensive functions of these families. The family myth for three generations was that men were to blame for everything that went wrong in the family, and that the women should support each other. The overriding family rule said that men were bad and aggressive, whereas subconsciously women chose men whom they could control. At the same time it gave the women leverage to keep their contact with the family of women close-knit and tight (Pillari 1994). Thus sex-role stereotypes are also created in the family of origin.

The family influence can also be experienced in

children's own sex-role identity, which can be confusing to them if they are made to feel different.

> After many years of trying, Madeline and her husband had a son. Madeline, who had hoped for a daughter, dressed the child as if he were a girl and did not cut his curly hair. Ultimately her husband, hearing people question his wife about her "daughter," got angry and took the 2-year-old for a haircut. Madeline cried all the way to the hairdresser: she did not want her son's hair to be cut because "he looked so pretty as a girl." Was there some degree of castration in this picture of a mother wanting her son to be a daughter? We do not know, except that as an adult in crisis the son turned to homosexuals for help and would sit in gay bars when he felt unhappy or unworthy. In therapy, he insisted that he was a heterosexual, but felt "safe" with homosexuals as they did not judge him.

Children learn how to become adults in the mosaic of family life. The manner in which children are parented helps them form the core beliefs about themselves. In families with many unresolved issues, such as alcoholism or marital infidelity, parents often say, in effect, "Do as I tell you but *do not* do what I am doing." Families that lack intimacy also create a invisible line around the family, which is referred to as a *subcultural boundary*. These boundaries contribute greatly to the invisible wall that surrounds the whole family, and help to keep the system closed. The dysfunctional family neither seeks nor accepts any new information that might break old beliefs or behavior patterns. In fact, they are afraid to do that and thus lead their lives in circular feedback loops.

Often these families have scandals, such as alcoholism in the family, that they do not want anyone to talk about.

> Leonard's father was murdered by his second wife about twenty years ago when he was unfaithful to her. This was published in the newspapers and everyone in the community was aware of it. The family made special efforts not to discuss it, however, and admonished anyone who brought it up. Leonard came for therapy when he was in his thirties because he continued to suffer from poor sleep and nightmares about his father's murder that he was afraid to talk about at home.

One of the most important factors in such families is control. They send messages to their children that say, "Don't ask questions!" The children learn not to ask because they will be frowned upon and punished.

When one has excessive need to control or deny, his or her feelings get lost. Being in control gives a person a sense of power, predictability, and security. Added to control are feelings of perfectionism, blame, denial of feelings, and a no-talk rule (Bradshaw 1988). In such families there is no discussion of crucial matters. The family sends out the message, "You must always be right in what you do." As a mother described her adult children, "They are perfect children, and will never do anything wrong," while her daughter was swindling her husband's family and her son was having an affair. The perfectionistic standard that is set up for the children may be about intellectual achievement, moral righteousness, or being upper class. The children have a standard imposed on them. There is a "one-up" or "we are better than others" aspect to this rule that covers the shame. The members in such families live according to an externalized image. Even as adults they may think in terms of "Am I pleasing my parents?" or "Am I living up to their expectations?" This leads to chronic dissociation from the true self. They are always busy self-monitoring and constantly asking themselves, "Am I coming across okay to my parents?" Comparing oneself to an external norm is a different way of being a person.

> As Edwin said in therapy, he was a perfect child who felt that he had to be very obedient and do all the chores in the family. This included being able to please his parents constantly. While the other 7-year-olds were having fun playing outside, Edwin would have to cut wood and take care of the yard. When there was anything wrong in the yard, he would be blamed. Young Edwin worked very hard at pleasing his parents. However, if anyone complained that the yard was not really well kept, the mother blamed the neighbors' children to her relatives, and insisted that she came from a "perfect family."

In this sense blame is used as a defensive cover-up for shame. A person's blaming behavior covers his or her shame or projects it onto others.

> When Trisha left her unfaithful husband, his sister insisted that he was unfaithful only because Trisha was offensive and ugly to look at, although Trisha as a teenager was the homecoming queen in her high school.

When a person is shame-based (avoiding negative feelings), then he or she cannot feel vulnerable or needy or ashamed, and blame becomes the automatic way to avoid the deepest feelings and also the true self. Blame maintains the balance in a dysfunctional system when control has been broken. But life is always unpredictable, and blame is used to regain the illusion of control. When one person feels the danger of shame and vulnerability, he or she will blame someone else.

> When Matilda was asked, "Why did you disinherit your daughter?" she blamed her daughter: "She said she didn't want anything," although the daughter had not spoken to her mother for three years after being disinherited by her.

Dysfunctional families deny their feelings, perceptions, thoughts, wants, and imaginings, especially the negative ones like fear, hurt, rejection, loneliness, sadness, and dependency. As Bradshaw (1988) puts it, they follow the perfectionist rule, which says, "You shouldn't think, feel, desire, imagine, see things, hear things, the way you do. You should see, hear, feel, think, imagine, desire the way the perfectionistic ideal demands" (p. 81). This is followed by the no-talk rule, which says that you do not talk openly about any feelings, thoughts, or experiences that focus on pain and loneliness and the negatives in the family system.

Denial of expression is toxic and creates its own dysfunction. Some families have myths that make them look only at the bright side, with the hope that everyone is distracted from what is really happening. For example, children in a family are aware that their father is having an affair. However, they are also told by the mother, "See how well we live . . . he is a good provider." An attempt to overlook problems. This family system is rigid and closed and no child has permission to question anything, that is, to rock the boat. In such families there is subtle chronic fighting and conflict without any real resolution.

There may also be a great deal of enmeshment, but never any genuine and mutual contact. Members thus are always upset and confused. There is also in such relationships no expectation of reliability. When you do not trust anyone, you will not be disappointed. Usually such people have not had their dependency needs met as children and they cover up their insatiability with fantasy-bonded illusions of self-sufficiency. Such people may act aloof and independent, developing rigid boundaries that preclude really intimate relationships, or they may be dependent and needy, which makes everyone feel incomplete and so they do not get their needs met in an appropriate manner. One of the worst problems of dysfunctionalism is that there are "open secrets" in the family that are beyond the denial system of the family, such as someone being arrested for murder and being incarcerated. The family is aware of this, but it keeps the family frozen. Everyone in the family is aware of these open secrets and everyone knows what everyone pretends not to know. In such families the saddest thing is that children and adults give up their ego boundaries as a way of maintaining the family system. When people give up their ego boundaries they have also given up their sense of self. These families are controlled by perfectionism and blame.

Because these children's first and most important relationships taught them that the people they love will hurt them and be terrifyingly unpredictable, most adult children of abusive parents, whether the abuse was physical, sexual, or emotional, are terrified of becoming close to another person. Successful adult relationships, whether between lovers or friends, require a significant amount of vulnerability, trust, and openness, the very elements that are destroyed in dysfunctional families. As a result, many adult children of dysfunctional families are drawn to people who are emotionally unavailable because of deep conflicts of their own. This pattern is often covered over with myths, secrecy, and strong fears of personhood, and when chanced upon in therapy, it is often a result of other issues, such as school problems or unemployment.

Hope is always prevalent when people decide to work on their issues in therapy and try to be honest with themselves and their issues. Without hope, no problems can really be dealt with.

> Forty-year-old Jason expressed no emotions in therapy. He came because of pressure from his wife. He told me he felt no emotions: "I am an unemotional man." He had no friends and no hobbies. With encouragement, he joined a men's group, yet there was no change in his behavior. Without emotion, he would mention cruel comments that his wife made to him; worse still, he would not confront her. He had been married for twenty-five years and was used to her way of treating him. In the group, however, the men made him dramatize what happened, which he did with their help. Finally he expressed his emotions with feeling while he hit a pillow and the group cheered. Another day, at home, he became angry when his wife insulted him and told her, "I will not take that kind of language from you." This marked the first encounter in which he had stood up for himself, and his smile was broad as he told the story. It was obvious he was becoming alive.
>
> After months of therapy and group sessions, Jason asked his son what he thought of him as a father. His son looked at his father and replied honestly, "I don't want to hurt your feelings, but you were never

there." Jason was shocked. He had been home every single day after work. When he asked how his son could even think in this manner, the boy replied that he had never seen his dad get angry or be upset, and that his dad did not seem to care about anybody or anything. When he heard this, Jason was very perturbed and doubled his efforts at being a person with feelings. In therapy, after thirty-nine years of being a nonemotional man, he broke down and cried. He was angry at himself for having been emotionally unavailable to his son and his family. With determination he worked at his emotions and there was an emotional growth spurt. He was finally becoming a person who could deal with his emotions and who had a sense of self. It appeared as if he was coming out of an emotional coma. With his recovery, there was also anger and bitterness about not having been alive for a long time. However, he made up for lost time through his friendships with other men and by doing things with them, and also by spending quality time with his wife and son and learning to express himself and be a "real person" again.

SEX-ROLE STEREOTYPING

Middle-class families often rear their children with stereotypical cultural and sexual values. In such families stoic males, oriented toward control with little access to feelings, are balanced by seductive, childlike females, who never confront others openly but utilize a number of manipulative techniques. In such families rules are created in terms of overt power differences, and define how children are to possess interpersonal power according to their sex. Although there is a belief in overt power differences according to the usual sexual stereotypes, other factors overshadow such behaviors. For instance, the father who feels inadequate may drink to the point of losing his job and then blame his family for his failures and difficulties. The mother resents staying at home, views her children as a burden, and desires to compete with men, confront danger, and seek excitement. In this case both the mother and the father feel guilty about their "defects" and verbally pass on to their children the same male/female standards and the same sense of guilt over not being able to live up to them.

Allen (1993) describes how men are taught to be men in our society. As a rule, little boys, more than little girls, are required to restrict their emotions. Men in our society are assigned three traditional roles: providing, protecting, and procreating. To fulfill these roles, little boys must suppress most of their emotions. Our culture (and many others) maintains that men are more efficient workers and warriors when they are not inconvenienced by tender emotions and feelings. To gain this end, boys are raised according to a masculine code that is a complex set of beliefs influencing the way we think, feel, and behave. The masculine code is not taught through institutional or formal means, but by boys and men absorbing the thousands of messages that filter down to them through parents, siblings, peers, ministers, teachers, scout leaders, comic books, cartoons, TV shows, action movies, and commercials (Allen 1993).

I remember training my son to fit in with modern society and to learn to be sensitive to men and women. I wanted him to overcome sexual stereotypes and be empathic to girls and boys. As a child of 2, he had both blue and pink shorts and shirts. He had both "girl's toys" and "boy's toys." I was supremely happy with the idea that he would grow up to be a talkative, sensitive, caring, and overtly affectionate young man. Alas, at age 3, after two days at a Montessori school, he came home declaring he would never again wear pink clothes because they were "girl's colors." He threw out the toys he thought were girls' toys, and before long I found in my young son a macho child, highlighting his masculinity and what he could do or not do depending upon what he heard at school from the teachers and his peers. One day my son came running home after playing in the garden with a friend to tell me he had been bitten by a snake. I panicked, but my 4-year-old laughed and reassured me that he did not have to go to a doctor because he had been bitten by a pregnant female snake and females do not hurt much, according to his friend. At this point I abandoned my ideas of unisex upbringing and let my son choose who he wished to be based upon family values and what he acquired in terms of masculinity from society. Children do not grow up solely in the home, although that influence is tremendous, but they become members of society as soon as they enter the school system, or even earlier if they are in daycare.

As Allen (1993) indicates, these messages from the outside world generally encourage boys to be competitive and focus on external success, rely on their intellect, withstand physical pain, and repress their vulnerable emotions. When boys attempt to violate the code of masculinity, it is not uncommon for them to be teased, shamed, or ridiculed. The purpose of this is not to cause emotional injury but rather to harden them to face difficulties men have always had to confront. The primary role of the man is that of provider for the family, and he rarely has the luxury of working when he pleases or selecting only those tasks that please him. The weather, the economy, and his boss dictate what he does, when he works, and how long he toils. Men buy into the cultural notion of external success as the manly road to happiness and security.

> When Jackson lost his job as a company chief executive officer, he refused to consider a lesser job; he felt he had reached the top at an early point in his career and did not wish to come down in status. This lasted for only a few months, however; Money began to be tight and his family suffered. Still he could not find any kind of work. Out of depression and his inability to talk about it to his wife or anyone else, Jackson attempted suicide. In therapy he said that it was unmanly to discuss feelings because if he had a job those feelings would go away.
>
> Simplistic thinking by Jackson, but it did fit the mold of being a man in society. Therefore, his coping and adapting capabilities were only tuned in as being part of the workforce; without a job, talking about feelings was useless.
>
> Allen (1993) describes a "Wildman" gathering; a male-bonding group in which men experience friendships and spend time together camping, rock climbing, and developing warrior skills. The group caters to men of all age groups and helps them build a community that lasts well beyond the outing. Allen asked men to reveal some of the messages they had received from their fathers or brothers while growing up and the response came quickly.

> "Don't feel."
> "Big boys don't cry."
> "There's nothing to cry about, think it through."
> "Get that look off your face!"
> "Tough it out."
> "Stop whining like a girl."

"Stop being a sissy."
"Be a man, get control of yourself."
"You're acting like a girl."

With these messages crowding in on them, boys learn not to express their emotions, and come to view women as emotional and men as rational.

The differences in communication styles between boys and girls begin at a young age. Boys are taught to compete and be dominant, girls to look for equality and intimacy. Thus there appear to be key conversational differences between men and women, derived from subcultural training. Women, for example, tend to ask questions as a way of maintaining a conversation, whereas men ask questions to request information.

Differences in men and women are vividly presented by Robert Sheldon (1982) in his offbeat poem:

You want me to understand
Your point.
And you want to understand
Exactly what I told you.
You would like to have IT ALL
crystal clear;
it should be clear;
understand, expressed completely,
specifically defined,
Repeated until it is vivid,
almost alive.
We must labor
until you are satisfied
that all the points
of the conversation
are clearly in your mind.
You're somehow comfortable

when all the ideas expressed
are absolutely clear to you.
And so, for you, this is done.
    We cleared it all up.
    We sorted it all out.
You now have all the points
    explicitly in mind.
You now understand me completely,
    and now I understand
exactly what you said to me.

You are satisfied.
It is all clear.

Now what?
[p. 55]

The poem tells us how men and women in everyday life view each other. However, matters can be worked through when people have created an intimate relationship in which there is love and respect for each other.

Healthy families are relatively free of the sexist role definitions that involve a totally macho man and an irrational woman. In healthy families there are also autonomy and individuation among family members; two people commit themselves to each other willingly. They *decide* and *choose* to stand by each other no matter what. A good relationship between two people is based on true love. It is not just a feeling—it is a *decision* (Bradshaw 1988). Thus, in a healthy family, parents tend to model their own self-discipline and self-love as well as their maturity and autonomy for their children.

Each parent feels "whole" as an individual and as

one-half of a couple. Rather than using their children to complete themselves, they are able to give of themselves to help their children become free to grow and use their own powers of knowing, loving, feeling, deciding, and imagining to accomplish their own individual self-actualization. The parents do not use the children to satisfy their own frustrations and anxiety-ridden projections. In marriages where intimacy is a basic aspect, couples have to work with each other to reach their individual balance, and, as mentioned, at times go beyond the cultural stereotypes of womanhood or manhood. In successful relationships the person should have freedom to pursue full self-acceptance and integration. For couples to be able to work at their sexual roles and differences, the therapist must create an atmosphere in which the woman can be open, assertive, or even directly angry, and the man can be tender, openly frightened, or uncertain. A woman who has been stereotyped as an hysterical female will not suddenly become assertive. At first her assertiveness is accompanied by hostility, as she tries to work through her image of a belittled person. A "compulsive" man who is power-oriented and unaware of feelings requires work to realize that women as well as men need to have confidence and substance in order to be lovable and trustworthy. Through therapy a man learns to listen to and respect the thoughts and wishes of his wife, not out of duty or responsibility but out of genuine caring and as a practical means of getting his own needs met. When people realize that gaining satisfaction is intimately related to giving satisfaction, they begin to understand many paradoxes of human existence (Beavers 1985).

In healthy relationships there is no strong myth of the domineering male or submissive female. Encouraging individual autonomy and responsibility is a necessary ingredient for the development of a happy family. In a family system in which there is substantial give and take, men and women are not at odds with each other and can function cooperatively. When people think in stereotypical ways, however, that can create conflicts or can represent projections of the tension within an individual onto the larger family group. Often these projections are overlooked or encouraged by unchallenged sexual stereotypes. However, as soon as people stop making assumptions, new learning can take place and new satisfactions can be obtained through broadening the definitions of maleness and femaleness. For instance, most fathers become comfortable and enjoy parenting when given a chance to do so. Mothers find a new joy in children when the fathers are actively involved and also begin to participate in children's interests beyond the home with excitement.

One of the stereotypical cultural myths about the unfulfilled woman occurs when she goes back to school over the "scared and bigoted objections" of her husband, who has to take on more responsibilities at home. Couples who view themselves in this oppositional fashion have not had the opportunity to function as individuals in various social situations. Depressed women and distant husbands are often similar in their pain or dissatisfaction. If a woman can define herself as a choice-making adult, her husband can receive more from her, but if she sees him as part of her difficulty, and he guiltily agrees of disagrees, the stage is set for projection, blame, and failure of resolution. In families all members need each other. When family tragedies happen there are no villains, only victims, and a system-oriented therapist will steadily break down sexual stereotypes that encourage false myths and false solutions.

The meek, mild, submissive wife often becomes

depressed. Her husband attempts to make her feel better but fails. In most treatment situations she will go through a radical change. From a submissive woman who works in the kitchen and takes care of all her husband's and children's needs, she becomes an "angry free woman" who sees all men as enemies. There is a projection of her introjected bad image culturally encouraged and transmitted by the family (Beavers 1985). If her needs, choices, and practical solutions are pointed out to her, however, she moves from her overaggressiveness to effective assertiveness. At this point the man's helpless guilt or rage can develop into a new appreciation of living with a verbal person rather than a compliant stranger.

> Lisa and Larry came for therapy at her insistence because she was troubled by his preoccupation with his work and his inability to communicate anything at home. Lisa in turn appeared to be childlike in manner, although she mentioned that she was capable of returning to college and getting her master's degree. She subtly added that she wished to go back to college and get her graduate degree because she thought that with only a bachelor's degree she could not get a decent job. Later she added that the idea of divorce had passed through her mind many times. Her husband, however, wanted to make the marriage work, and found her sudden desire to go back to college very threatening. He appeared more threatened when she mentioned that she had been toying with the idea of divorce. At this point Lisa burst into an angry tirade, pointing out his faults, such as his emotional distance and selfishness. The therapist helped Lisa reduce the intensity of her attacks so that her husband, who was easily fright-

> ened by her demands, would be willing and able to understand her and her desires. With the therapist's help Lisa started to explain to him how her life felt like a vacuum and she needed to do more than just be a housewife. In the course of therapy the therapist found that Larry reacted to Lisa in predictable ways. Depending upon how she talked to him, he varied from warmth to withdrawal. As she saw him listen carefully and become more empathic, her earlier feelings of anger and frustration were replaced with positive feelings. She commented that they needed each other. After many sessions she said that she still wanted her master's degree but did not wish to divorce her husband. At this point he reassured her with positive feedback. They began to communicate and trust each other and expressed enjoyment in companionship.

Why do people have so many problems with reference to gender differences? Most of them not only believe that men and women differ, but also share similar beliefs about the differences. Beliefs of this sort, which are based upon oversimplification or overgeneralization, are called *stereotypes*. As Masters and colleagues (1988) indicate, stereotypes can be harmful because they lead to erroneous judgments and generalizations that affect how people treat one another.

In one sense, masculinity and femininity refer to the degree to which a person matches cultural beliefs of how males and females should behave and look. A woman is expected to be tender, shy, and always loving and caring; a man is seen as work-oriented and does not talk about feelings. However, research findings by Masters and Johnson (1988) have shown that the view of masculinity and femininity as opposites is incorrect, as both sides coexist in every individual. Thus it can be said that a woman who is competitive can also be quite feminine, and a man who is tender and loving can also be very masculine. It is helpful to look at people in this fashion so that we do not get caught in stereotypes.

Gender roles in most societies have a strong impact on sexual attitudes and behavior. For example, in the United States it is thought that males are innately more interested in sex than females, that men characteristically assume an active role and that females are passive. These stereotypes have some behavioral consequences and women often accept the notion that they are not to initiate sex, even in a romantic married situation.

When we look at another culture that has a different set of expectations about sexual interaction we can understand how limiting stereotypes can be. In Mangaia, a tiny Polynesian island in the South Pacific, the cultural message is that sexual pleasure is for everyone. As a result, there are few if any boys and girls who have not had substantial sexual experience prior to marriage (Marshall 1971).

What we need to understand is that with stereotypes also grow family relationships with children, who in turn learn ideas of men and women based upon their own life experiences, which of course tremendously influence their life choices, decisions, and behaviors. The manner in which a man or woman presents himself or herself in a relationship can lead to a relationship that is healthy or unhealthy.

POWER AND VULNERABILITY ISSUES

There are taboos and realities in every family, and children grow up either questioning and understanding events in the family or responding to the silent message that says in effect, "Do not ask questions because you will not get answers."

In some families communication among family members is based upon manipulation, evasion, and masking, because there is a need to pretend and cover up problematic issues.

> Joy was raped at 13 by her uncle, but this was never discussed in the family, nor was her fear of her uncle discussed. His behavior was dismissed as immaturity. As Joy was unwilling to get involved with a man, her mother arranged a blind date with a young man she had met at a store. Although Joy was only in her early twenties, her family's myth said that girls should get married young. Thus Joy had a number of blind dates, but no steady boyfriend. Finally it appeared that one blind date would lead to wedding bells. There was a great deal of manipulation by the mother for Joy to pursue the young man, although Joy really did not like him. In fact, she was terrified of his voice as it reminded her of the men in her family, loud and boisterous. However, he appeared to be caring and did little things to please her. With the burden of being a spinster in a family that did not believe that women could live on their own, Joy agreed on their seventh date to marry Tim. Thus began a relationship, more to please her family than to satisfy her own needs. Even during the dating period Joy allowed Tim to decide everything they should do. Tim was pleased. He saw Joy as not being a strong person and enjoyed being in charge and taking care of her. After a few months of marriage Joy felt stifled by the sexual act, and by the close, tight relationship in which Tim wanted to discuss everything. Joy was not used to discussing every-

> thing in her family of origin and thus began their first power struggle. When Joy returned from work, she had to get the home to look clean and have dinner ready on the table and listen to all that Tim had to say—and he talked endlessly.
>
> Joy, who was not used to direct communication, attempted to put him off by pretending to be asleep and by not listening. In the process she found out things he did not like, and made it a point to do those things, such as cooking vegetables he hated, and then pretending that she did not remember his dislike, being "too busy" to talk or listen to him, and by developing "headaches" in bed. Although Tim was loud, he was not a mean person and would give in to Joy when she complained of not feeling well. Tim's mother had died young and Tim was terrified of people being sick. Joy used his weakness to manipulate him. The more her awareness of his weakness grew, the more she used it, including not going to work, sleeping late, and complaining that she was ill. This was the only time Tim was not boisterous and would look out for her. While he manipulated her with his loudness, she learned to manipulate him with her "illnesses," which created the distance she needed to keep their communication at a minimum. In different ways each one of them had power and used each other's vulnerability to create and maintain their power.

All families and partners in families have power struggles. According to Haley (1963), people in relationships are always struggling to define or redefine the relationship to meet their own goals or needs. He classifies relationships as *symmetrical* when both communicators have equal status, or *complementary* when one gives and the other receives. In symmetrical relationships couples tend to be fairly competitive, as they both wish to survive the symmetry. Maneuvers are used to change the relationship. For example, when a person seeks medical help, the physician makes a diagnosis and prescribes treatment. However, when the patient begins to ask questions about the side effects and other aspects of the treatment plan, questioning the doctor might be viewed as an attempt to "maneuver" or change the relationship from a complementary one to a symmetrical one. There are a large number of maneuvers that we use in dealing with people to preserve or alter a particular power relationship.

In relationships there is also overt and covert power. If, in a relationship, one person exercises more overt power against a partner, the partner may battle toe to toe to resist, or appear to submit while moving to redress the power balance through covert methods, as Joy did through her illness. It is axiomatic that the less overt power a person has, the more covert are his or her attempts to gain control. When two people are unable to share overt power equally, they will be caught up in an endless, frustrating struggle with no winners, or the partner who both agree is the more powerful will win every battle but will feel overly responsible and emotionally deprived (Beavers 1985).

> Virginia was overcontrolling of her husband, Herman, who was unemployed and depended upon her for everything. Instead of allowing him to struggle through his unemployment and find a job himself, his wife took it upon herself to call the employment agencies and read the help-wanted advertisements, completed application forms on his behalf, and called prospective employers to find him a job.

> Herman resented what Virginia was doing and said so, but she did not listen. Herman was unemployed for two years, as he covertly sabotaged every interview and job opportunity his wife found for him.

Nobody likes to feel powerless, not even in abusive relationships, so when equality disappears, then one partner has to regain the power in the relationship. For true intimacy a relationship of equality is necessary. This equality of power has to be experienced by both or it does not exist. Experiencing intimacy and sharing thoughts and feelings that make a person vulnerable become impossible when there is a perceived power difference that provides an atmosphere of resentment and anxiety, precluding openness and sharing. In troubled relationships in which there is an unequal sharing of power, the stronger partner views the weaker much as a parent would view a child. However, they still attempt to obtain objectives though intimidation, direct, angry, attacks, and judgmental "shoulds." As Beavers (1985) indicates, becoming nonfunctional, for example, being in bed and pretending an illness, or being irrational, childlike, or suicidal, are reverse ways of intimidating a person.

> Art and Betsy were in therapy because Art had an affair while he was unemployed. They ended their therapy after a couple of years as they moved to a new town. Art made a special effort to find a job but did not succeed. Betsy was very irritable, as she wanted everything to begin well in the new area. She began to nag him every day, complaining that he was still unemployed and a burden on her resources. Art got back at her by visiting a prostitute and leaving signs at home to show that he was being unfaithful. This was a cruel but covert way of

showing that he was struggling to create equality in power by upsetting his wife and making her think through her own actions in terms of put-downs that she used against her husband.

It is important to understand that intimacy can be minimal when couples come from dysfunctional families of origin and have never experienced a respectful or meaningful relationship.

BOUNDARY DISTURBANCES AND AMBIVALENCE

Most boundary problems arise because of expectations and goals that families create for themselves. For example, a single mother allows her sons to sleep in her bed as they join her to watch TV. When she remarries, her second husband objects to the boys going into his bedroom.

Visher and Visher (1988) identified three types of boundaries: personal boundaries, couple boundaries, and intergenerational boundaries. *Personal boundaries* are what we carry with us in our personal space. In a marriage they depend upon how husband and wife treat each other. There is wide variation in the amount of personal space and privacy needed by individuals. In some marriages women who have learned that it is important to be dependent upon the man may appear to be clingy; however, in their own family of origin this is acceptable and thus they expect it to be the same with a partner. The period of dating is unnatural, as each partner puts their best foot forward. However, after the marriage, when the wife continues to be clingy, the husband reacts to it by encouraging and rewarding that type of behavior or by being critical, disgusted, and distant in the marriage.

> Watching her husband distance himself from her was the most painful experience in Ellen's life. Bob was a handsome, well-educated man and she had not expected to do so well in her marriage, since she was seen as the "loser" in her family of origin. Afraid that Bob's good looks would attract other women, she became more and more clingy. This irritated her husband, who in turn started to spend more time with the boys at the bar. As time passed, he stayed away for longer periods of time. Although Ellen had a house and three young children to look after, as well as a part-time job, she tried to keep a watch on her husband by telephoning him ten to fifteen times a day. When he finally lost patience, he had his secretary tell his wife he was busy. The inevitable happened—Bob had an affair. This devastated Ellen and she was confused about how to deal with the problem. She thought of divorce, but with three children and a part-time job she could not manage. Therapy was suggested by a few friends, and Ellen finally got the courage to make the necessary phone calls, but her husband refused to see a therapist. Her constant reminders of his affair and his resistance to therapy was *her power* over him. Her reminders finally caused him to lose control and he began to curse and hit her. This physical and verbal abuse were the worst forms of violations of her rights as a person and as a wife. Because he pushed her around and hit her, he began to violate her personal boundaries as a free human being.

There are many such cases in which, because of unresolved difficulties in marital or partner relationships, one partner violates the rights of another in a direct and overt fashion.

Questions of new boundaries also come into play when there are newly formed families.

> Ike was an only child until he was 11 years old. When his mother remarried there were three more additions to their home: the stepfather and his two sons. Suddenly Ike had to share his bedroom with a younger stepbrother. Ike found every place in the house crowded: the den with the TV, or the bathroom, to the point that each person had to ask the others before they could decide who could go in first and how much time he could spend. This really threw Ike off, as he was used to being an only child. He got tired of the constant loud talking and screaming in the house. He felt that he had no privacy and this bothered him. He constantly complained to his mother and, luckily, as his school grades were beginning to drop, Ike's mother and stepfather worked toward giving Ike more personal space by providing him with his own study.

Setting *couple boundaries* is fairly easy when it is a first marriage for both people, provided that the personal boundaries of each individual were respected in their families of origin. However, problems can occur in subsequent marriages or relationships, particularly when there are small children. Forming a solid couple bond is more difficult in stepfamilies as many different issues need to be handled at the same time. The couple is adjusting to a new marriage, dealing with former spouses, and attempting to keep the household running smoothly. Nourishing the couple relationship seems crucial to the success of the new family. There are usually two blocks to the couple relationships: (1) an adequate boundary around the couple, and (2) the remarried parent's guilt and fear over losing the relationship with children. Some parents believe that by developing an intimate and emotionally close relationship with their new partners they betray their children and destroy the earlier relationship they had with them. Children who have spent too much time with their single mother or father may also be possessive of them and may wish to sabotage the new relationship if they realize that they have the power to do so. This is not because children are bad, but because they are loyal to the absent parent and do not wish to see a new person take over.

Boundary problems may be created in several ways. One, as noted, might be that the young children are used to sleeping in their mother's bed or cuddling up to her before falling asleep. They see the stepfather as an intruder and are unhappy when they are not able to continue the old habits. If they persist, the new father feels left out, like an outsider, with the mother and children cozying up to each other. In such situations children react to their stepparent with resentment and anger if they are not prepared sufficiently for this new relationship.

Another example of a boundary problem is the situation of a person who has divided loyalties between his or her children from the former spouse and the new spouse's children.

> The precipitating event that brought Victor and Jo into therapy was the trip that Victor was planning with his own son and daughter without consulting his new wife and her two children. To Jo's angry questioning he responded that he felt he had neglected his own children and felt guilty. He decided

that the only way to make it up to them was to take them on a nice vacation without any "intrusion" from his new family. Jo was angry and hurt. She felt second best next to his own biological children. When she attempted to change his mind, he said that his children would be disappointed.

In therapy Victor's lack of commitment to his new wife and marriage and his deep attachment to his children became very clear. There were also quarrels between Jo's son and his stepfather. Finally, with no resolution reached, it looked as though the marriage was ready to crumble as Jo talked about not wanting to be in a marriage where she was not consulted or treated like a partner. At this point Victor broke his emotional reserve and, struggling to withhold tears, blurted out that he did not want to give up his relationship with his own children for a relationship with his new wife and children. Jo understood his dilemma and explained that she did not want to disrupt his relationship with his own children and understood his fear of losing them. At this point the couple began to work together, seriously talking and working through different issues that concerned them. Slowly their bonds began to strengthen and they did not threaten each other with divorce again. Victor started to bring his biological children home, and Jo and her two children got to know all of them and care about each other. As their relationship blossomed, tensions in the household subsided and they began to work well as a couple. There was a reworking of the boundaries, and Jo's children began to respect the new boundaries that were being created. The children learned, for example, to knock and ask if they could enter the parents' bedroom without rushing in as they formerly did.

Intergenerational boundaries with cross-generational myths arise when the parents' marriage is based on mutual distortions, and children may be linked to the marital collusion by processes of recruitment. For example, a mother and her daughter talk about the father as being a "weak" man. The daughter learns to ridicule the father because she has the support and encouragement of the mother, who has problems with her husband, dislikes him but cannot leave him as she is economically dependent upon him, and therefore chooses her young, dependent daughter as a friend and partner in ridiculing her husband.

Many times marital defenses are created around factors like genital sexuality and violence. An older woman who came from a moralistic home married an alcoholic who beat and abused her. She repeatedly told her daughter that "men are bad and sex is repulsive." As the children grew older they learned to dislike men and sex. It created maturational problems for the children, and one daughter had been in therapy for a long time (Pillari 1994).

The lack of clear intergenerational boundaries is likely to interfere with the younger person's emotional development and lead to problems in marriage later on.

> A mother loved her son, Henry, very much. When he was 15 she decided that she did not want to lose him to another woman and therefore did all she could to create a strong bond between them. This was done by asking her son to go to the store and buy her bras and panties.
>
> When he protested she would say, "I'm your mother and I feel you should do it." The embarrassed teenager purchased his mother's intimate clothing. Many years later in therapy he mentioned

that he never forgot his mother's bra size and compared it to that of the women he dated. Thus a cross-generational, seductive relationship was created by the mother, who believed they were a close family and saw the son as her property. Although she had a daughter she did not ask her daughter to buy her bras and panties.

Henry was confused in the initial stages of therapy, as he was overwhelmed by the power of his mother and had problems seeing the family as dysfunctional. After a number of sessions, he realized that there were a number of myths in the family about love and togetherness, and his mother's role was to pretend that they were all very close to each other. After years of therapy, Henry realized that his mother wanted to seduce him and keep him as her own. In some ways she succeeded. It took Henry a long time to fall in love and marry, which he did in his mid-thirties. He realized that the closeness his mother felt toward him was rather dysfunctional when she told him on his wedding day that he had to share all the details of his marriage with her every day. He politely refused.

The family consensus image can lead to impoverished family life with family myths that give similar roles to family members. "We are a happy/intellectual/quiet family." If this is based upon the capacity to enjoy life and deal with angry or conflictual situations constructively, then it is not a myth, but if the family cannot tolerate ambivalence and denies the consensus script, and also hides the opposite feared or taboo drama, then it may become a family myth that is too carefully followed by all family members (Byng-Hall 1973).

Cross-generational myths can be built in different

ways. In the first case the family went out of their way to choose men who would discredit them, and then made men the stigmatized scapegoats. It appears there was a marital collusion between husband and wife about the different roles they could play. The women chose men who would become their personal scapegoats. This drew the women even closer, and they treated the men as outsiders. The men colluded in this management by playing the role of ne'er-do-well, drinking, gambling, and carousing. A person labeled as weak, dangerous, or bad is diminished from a whole individual worthy of respect to a tainted, discounted person with reduced power in the family system.

Only when there are situations of more or less equal power can there be true intimacy, that is, the experience of being open and vulnerable and able to share one's innermost feelings and thoughts. At any age overt power and intimacy are highly correlated. When there is unequal overt power, the top dog is fearful of exposing weakness and the bottom dog is fearful that his or her anger, assertiveness, and wishes for equality or domination will surface and create problems. Thus each is necessarily isolated from the other to a significant degree (Beavers 1985).

The sexual encounter is usually the best, or the most dramatic, example of the relationship between power and intimacy. In intimate relationships complementarity and role differentiation appear necessary to allow emotional interaction with shared dignity. For example, when playing football, baseball, or cricket on unskilled teams, everyone tries to get the ball and the result is chaos, but on teams with skilled players the members have complementary roles (that is, different positions) and cooperate with each other.

In healthy relationships both partners need to be aware of the difference between one person's feelings and wishes and another's. This awareness is extremely important in working together, making decisions that can be accepted and supported by both with the "loser" still feeling good. When there are problems with healthy couples the boundaries may be fluctuating. A stubborn insistence on maintaining rigid boundaries is likely to be an indication of pathology in relationships. In positive relationships the boundaries may be lost in the midst of passion, whether angry or ecstatic. Sometimes the merging is delightful and sometimes it can be horrendous. When the relationship is healthy, the fortunate couple regroups, clears up the boundaries, and reestablishes effective dialogue between the two sovereign persons.

In unhealthy family situations, where there is no intimacy, the power situation is very different. As in cases of sexual abuse, there is violation of trust by sexualizing the relationship with the child and there is lack of intimacy and trust in the marriage. In such marriages there is also substantial guilt. For example, a person can take responsibility for his or her behavior without blaming others for life's tragedies, with reasonable self-acceptance. This reflects relatively less guilt about being assertive in a couple relationship. In homes where there is sexual abuse *triangles* are created. A triangle is an unhealthy three-way relationship in which there is little spontaneity. The relationships tend to be part of a closed system with rigid movements. What may appear as closeness among family members is actually *fusion*. In fusion one person overlaps the other so that there is a blurring of self-identification or self-differentiation. Unfortunately, this happens in incest relationships. As we are aware, there is no true consent, equality, respect, trust, or safety between family members. The overlapping that happens in incest confuses family members' boundaries and the different aspects of two people's inner lives and behaviors. Often, the incest victim is made to believe that he or she had a role in operating this forbidden sexual relationship.

For such children, and for the offender too, it is frequently difficult to tell where self ends and the other begins. Often, fusion and violated boundaries have happened in the family of origin. Triangles in families are not simply mechanical events but are often complex interactions that have both personal (intrapsychic) and relationship origins, dynamics, experiences, and meanings. In family triangles where children are the victims, the original, unresolved conflict and pain of the adult person from the fused unhealthy family of origin have not been worked through. In triangles there is a lost, hurting self that grows from the wound the adult self experienced as a child. Such people are experts at creating unhealthy boundaries. They become good at scapegoating different family members and act out compulsive behaviors and use them quite often, unconsciously, as a way of avoiding closeness and intimacy in a relationship where lack of intimacy would be appropriately a cause and a result of the triangles.

Every effort was made to obtain permission to reproduce the poem by Robert Sheldon cited in this chapter. The poem appears in his book *Relationships*, published in 1982 by Creative Communications Co. of Virginia Beach, VA. The author will be pleased to correct any error or omission that may be pointed out.

CHAPTER FIVE

Treatment Issues

In treatment we move toward understanding and working through the different issues that effectively diminish or destroy intimacy. People who are incapable of developing or maintaining intimacy in significant relationships have not resolved the original conflict, pain, or mistrust that they developed in their earlier relationships. They are carrying a "lost, hurting self." In the process they may have also developed unhealthy boundaries with much inner and outer confusion, pain, and chaos. These factors contribute to the avoidance of closeness and intimacy and create other symptoms and problems. One of these is *scapegoating*.

In scapegoating, a common phenomenon in a family, a specific person is chosen by the family to blame for its pain. Without intimacy, it is easy to scapegoat a child and blame him or her for all the pain in the family, while maintaining the unhealthy distancing that is the underlying cause of the problem. Intimacy is often thrown out the window because the family is so busy dealing with the pain of different issues that they forget that developing closeness can be the beginning of a solution to their problems. However, for people who have been brought up to believe that they cannot trust anyone, to open up and talk about how they feel is scary when their vulnerability has been used against them in the past. There are so many everyday examples, as seen in the case below.

> Bruce and Elsie avoid marital strife by focusing on their son's problems. Bruce complains that his son, Mike, watches too much TV and does not complete his homework. In the same breath he adds that Mike does not do his household chores, cannot turn on the TV for his baby sister when she cries or keep an eye on her, and the worst part is that he has "bad" friends. As soon as the father is out of the house, however, the mother, who has a number of issues with her husband, avoids the marital strife by developing an overcloseness with Mike. Both of them view the father as their common enemy. The stage is set for farther and son to avoid dealing with their distance and mistrust by relating to each other indirectly through the mother.

In this situation there is no clear victimizer or victim. When there are unhealthy boundaries, family members develop an inability to look at the drawbacks of their transactions and this is perpetuated in other relationships as well. A son who has been distanced from his own father and overly close to his mother may not know how to develop a relationship with his children or how to develop intimacy with his wife, especially if he has not been able to separate himself emotionally from his mother as an adult. With intimacy limited in a marriage, the ground is set for more unresolved issues and problems in the new or next generation as well. These can include anger, guilt, and the pain of deception in their own relationships.

There are different levels of intimacy and different layers of barriers to intimacy. Working through these layers needs to be done with care and caution, with the goal of achieving an understanding of self, a love of oneself, and the beginning ability to relate to others with comfort.

ANGER

When intimacy is broken in a relationship, the people involved are likely to be angry. If anger is not allowed to come out in constructive ways, it presents itself in difficult and unpleasant ways. If you ignore your hurt and anger, hoping they will go away, they will usually come back in stronger and more painful forms. There are three different ways of dealing with anger, as identified by Carlson (1981): "don't make waves," the "stamp saver," and the "silent approach."

The *"don't make waves"* anger occurs when people need to have peace at any price. The person will take the blame for anything, even things he or she did not do. Such a person is self-effacing and never appears angry. Often the peaceful demeanor is a sham. This person may have psychosomatic complaints, such as head- or stomachaches to dissipate the anger.

Another person may camouflage his or her anger by becoming a *"stamp saver."* This person will act like a martyr and collect a number of injustices. Eventually there will be an outburst in which every grievance, real or imagined, collected over the entire length of the relationship, will come out.

In the *silent approach* the person suddenly retreats into an icy silence when something is bothering him or her. When asked if something is wrong he or she will often flatly deny it, but somehow will manage to let everyone know he or she is upset by making sarcastic or grumpy remarks.

People with these kinds of symptoms are too uncomfortable or too threatened to deal with the underlying feelings, and the unconscious mind tries to do them a favor by channeling their bottled-up emotions into more acceptable form, such as physical symptoms.

In addition to the bottled-up emotions there are more obvious emotional symptoms, such as depression, neuroses, psychoses, and the potential for murder and suicide. This is not to say that unresolved hurts and anger are the sole cause of all mental and physical illness, but they are certainly contributing factors.

About 60 percent of all homicides occur among family members or in other close relationships where feelings are most apt to erupt. The victim is usually a spouse, lover, or friend, and the most likely place is the home. People who do not know how to deal with small amounts of anger may build up a reservoir of unresolved anger. Often one slight provocation is enough to fill the anger reservoir to the top and make them overflow (Carlson 1981). Unlike camouflaging, which is common among covertly angry persons, an overtly angry person may be chronically hostile or may only have occasional violent bursts of anger.

> Shaun was very upset with his boss but would not allow the anger to show. Instead, he got angry with his wife and son when he found they had eaten

dinner before he arrived. The fact that he was three hours late for dinner was of no consequence. He assumed that he had the right to be treated as the head of the family, especially since his self-esteem had been shattered at work.

Shaun, a short-tempered, impulsive person, would become furious over small things and could not deal with his anger in any constructive way. He created problems at home by taking out his frustrations on his family. At work he yelled and cursed at his subordinates, which complicated the situation. Shaun exacerbated his problems when he suddenly left his job. This placed a tremendous burden on him and his family, and brought him close to suicide. While it is helpful to express anger constructively, in Shaun's case his uncontrolled rage was a destructive force in his and in his family's life.

When looking at ways to handle anger, it is useful to place people on a continuum from the most to the least mature. The *most mature* person is always aware of his or her feelings and is able to determine their cause accurately. He or she deals with issues as they arise. Such a person frequently engages in strenuous physical activity as an outlet so that his or her negative feelings do not harm others. He or she has no significant accumulation of anger, and annoyances that bother other people seldom bother him or her.

The *somewhat mature* person is aware of his or her feelings of anger and is often aware of the primary feelings that caused it. He or she attempts to deal quickly with the problem and may either cover up the feelings or talk about them. This person may have a small amount of unresolved anger. Such persons occasionally bury some feelings that should be dealt with or blow up slightly when expressing feelings of hurt or anger. At times people may hear this person yell, but usually he or she will remedy the situation and apologize when appropriate.

The *somewhat immature* person is usually aware of his or her primary feelings of anger but only occasionally knows the specific causes for them. He or she occasionally attempts to deal with his or her feelings constructively but at other times deals with them destructively. These persons do not injure others physically, but may cause a fair amount of emotional hurt to those around them. They also collect a moderate fund of anger. These persons may be simply neurotic and have psychosomatic complaints, marital problems, and other difficulties. They may sulk and be passive-aggressive, but externally they look fairly well adjusted to all but those who are extremely close to them. These persons can lose their tempers, slam doors, and even break things in their attempts to give vent to their anger.

The *immature* person handles anger more poorly than people in other categories. Often such persons have a lot of guilt and depression in their lives and may be numb to their feelings. Such people rarely say what they feel and will not share their feelings honestly with others. They hide their anger in order to avoid conflict, only to have the effects emerge later in indirect ways. The overtly angry person is also prone to launch an angry counterattack and can often confuse issues and leave others hurt.

The *very immature* person is chronically angry and may try to hide his or her anger. Such a person has problems handling anger and is obviously hostile and physically abusive to those who get in the way. Normally he or she causes others much unhappiness and is a very unhappy person. Such people often use alcohol and have trouble with the law. They may feel guilty and depressed, and the feelings that haunt them can lead them to commit suicide or homicide. Such a person may be totally unaware that anger is a problem for him or her, and thus handles it destructively. Usually the person does not intend to hurt anyone but his or her problems are so great that it is virtually impossible for him or her to avoid creating problems for others as well. If not extremely depressed, he or she is emotionally numb. There may be neurosis or psychosis. People know that he or she is trouble, and without a drastic change the anger may turn to depression and hopelessness of such great magnitude that it can result in suicide.

Often the angry person feels ripped off by life and is constantly getting even, remembering every injustice that was done to him or her. Such people usually delight in the shortcomings of others and can be overly competitive. Angry people are often stuck with feelings of anger and use blame, which becomes a cover-up for feelings of inadequacy.

> Daniel had worked hard to provide for his parents and siblings. However, when his father died he was treated very shabbily by his mother. Feeling deeply hurt and unworthy of love and support, he would not turn to others for help. He drank to excess, seeing that as a way of dealing with his pain. After four years of drinking he found himself no longer employable in his profession, and was angry for letting himself go so low. His only true love, his wife, wanted a divorce because he refused to communicate with her, and with lack of intimacy in the relationship everything went downhill quickly despite therapy. With one leg out the door, he felt abandoned and angrier.

All human beings face anger at one time or another in their lives. How a person deals with it and works through it is important because unworked anger, as presented, can come out in different kinds of physical and mental problems.

ANXIETY

How can we define anxiety? Anxiety may be a constructive emotion when it motivates us to strive for excellence, but it may be an undesirable emotion when it immobilizes us and is experienced as distress or tension. Anxiety is different from fear, which usually signifies the presence of a known danger. The strength of fear is more or less proportionate to the degree of danger. Fear is a desirable emotion, and it leads to much that is useful—avoiding danger, for example (Goodwin 1986).

The absence of intimacy in relationships can lead to anxiety.

> Elizabeth feels a need to keep track of what her spouse, Albert, is doing because he has been unfaithful to her. She constantly searches his wallet, and calls him at work and at play just to reassure herself. Elizabeth is painfully anxious because there is no trust in the relationship and the couple is stuck with each other for financial reasons and for the sake of the children. She has never worked outside the home and feels diffident, insecure, and afraid to do so.

There is normal anxiety and abnormal anxiety. Everyone recognizes that abnormal anxiety is not good. For example, when a woman panics in a grocery store for no apparent reason, that is not normal. Worrying about her relationship with her boyfriend because matters are not going right for her seems more realistic and might be called normal anxiety.

Extreme anxiety because of past relationship failures becomes apparent when a person develops new relationships. Anxiety also creates suspicion and anger. When anxiety is related to pain, it carries with it other feelings of fear, anger, self-doubt, and insecurity; such feelings can be very hurtful to a person.

> Kitty was 30 years old and under pressure by her family to get married. Her father lamented that he sent her to the best college so that she could find herself a husband, and he could not understand why she was not married. It was true that Kitty had the best education but what her parents did not realize was that Kitty was afraid of commitment because she witnessed the problems that her parents had. Her father had been unfaithful to his wife a few times and had taken his grown sons on a night out and brought home a young girl in a drunken state. This angered Kitty's mother and there were quarrels about this incident for a long time. Kitty continued to hear about the incident until she left home to go to college. While at college, she constantly heard her parents talk about the "ideal man" she would bring home. This was sufficient to turn her off. Kitty was afraid of intimacy and love. She had seen her parents' relationship fall apart due to her father's open infidelities. Her relationships with the opposite sex were marked by fear, mistrust, insecurity, and a high degree of anxiety because she wanted so much to be what her father wanted her to be, a successful woman, which meant that she had to get married. As soon as Kitty went out with a man

whom she thought her parents would approve of, she would be on the phone checking up on him, even after the first date. A good thing would soon turn sour. Although Kitty continued the phone calls with any good dates, she seemed incapable of being intimate with the man. To her, sadly, intimacy meant being in a sexual relationship, which she saw as a way of receiving and giving love. However, the men in her life saw it as a physical act with no commitment, since they were not in love with her. In therapy her anger against the expectations that had been placed on her by her family came out in anxious, angry, painful tears. Kitty had lived for her parents, particularly her father, whose respect and love she wanted, but in therapy she learned that she had to live her life to fulfill her own dreams and goals rather than her parents' goals. She had to work through the pain she saw in her family, as her parents had a superficial marriage with money the glue that kept them together. The most important issues Kitty had to work through were her anxiety and anger with her father for being unfaithful to her mother, and the residue of feelings that the entire family shared. Kitty also had feelings of guilt when she was really happy, since she was the mother's confidante and was tied to her mother's issues of unhappiness in the marriage. Thus intimacy seemed far away, while issues in her family of origin overwhelmed her.

GUILT AND PRETENSE

In committed relationships and marriages, guilt develops when the emotional and sexual exclusivity is broken and the reactions of the betrayed mate are shock, anger, panic, and incredulity. The marriage no longer exists as a source of security, and suddenly there is no haven in the heartless world. A fiery storm of emotions takes over and there are accusations on the part of the faithful partner and defense, guilt, and anger on the part of the unfaithful partner.

Not many people are improved by guilt. In fact, most people are at their absolute worst when they feel guilty. Guilt is uncomfortable, and guilty people can experience fear and anger and identify the source as the person they felt guilty about hurting. As Pittman (1989) indicates, this strange phenomenon of hurting the person who makes them feel guilty is the root cause of infidelity. It is a carryover from adolescence, and happens in the following manner. A child does normal sexual things that have been driven underground by the parents, and alternates between guilt over a defined misdeed and anger at the parents for defining something so pleasurable as forbidden. The child is uncomfortable, as such an act is forbidden by the parents, which ultimately leads to confusion. The notion arises that what is forbidden must be fun. Therefore, when a person is feeling either pleasure or guilt, the appropriate response is anger at whoever caused the confusion between the two, whoever is witness to the guilty deed, and whoever is fueling the guilt.

It is also common for guilt-ridden people, after being unfaithful, to distance their unsuspecting mate, whose love makes the guilt-ridden feel even guiltier. Pittman (1989) indicates that the greater the discomfort and the more trusting the mate, the greater the distance needed to protect the unfaithful partner from being overwhelmed by guilt. The irony of this situation is that the unfaithful spouse will seek out the only person who can relieve this guilt—the accomplice in the act, the one who can assure that no wrong was done. In this manner the unfaithful spouse and the illicit lover are trapped behind imaginary enemy lines, hiding from the faithful partner who somehow gets turned into the source of painful guilt. This guilt undermines the marriage and fuels the affair.

> Alor and Mary Jean were married after a whirlwind courtship. Mary Jean was very accomplished, like her husband, and could stand on her own in every way. Alor loved her very much but was possessive and jealous when she went out of state to meetings and conferences. Often, in spite of his own busy schedule, he would accompany her and sit in on her luncheons with colleagues. He invariably pointed out some man who was overly attracted to Mary Jean, who was tired of his jealousy and tried to help him understand that her relationship was purely professional. Nevertheless, Alor began to neglect his work and accompanied his wife whenever she went on conferences. He frequently told her that someone was interested in her and she seemed not to mind, which led to fights between them. Finally the inevitable happened—Mary Jean had an affair. While Alor experienced pain and fury, Mary Jean became overly guilty and they divorced. Her investment in the marriage was limited. What happened in this marriage was that jealousy had become frighteningly inappropriate and intrusive. Where Alor felt like a couple, Mary Jean did not, and his possessiveness drove her "out of her mind." Such an imbalanced pattern inevitably destroyed their relationship and marriage.

Some adults are trained to admit nothing. By behaving in unacceptable ways, the deceptive partner begins to feel better. The faithful partner may feel hurt and take a one-down position; the unfaithful partner feels that he or she has a power advantage, and this is the betrayer's motivation in having an affair. Quite often this leads to the old scenario of lack of intimacy in the marriage.

> Paula separated from her husband, James, after forty years of marriage and moved to a new area to pursue her own interests. In therapy she said that she had four children and was economically dependent upon her husband. James was furious when she got pregnant the fourth time because he did not want another child. Although Paula claimed she had become pregnant accidentally, he did not believe her and was furious. Since then, their sexual life was limited and he began having affairs. Paula heard about it from her neighbors and her relatives but he always denied it. In disgust, Paula gave up and lived in the marriage until her children became adults. Her anger was overwhelming, and she said that she had hated him for years.

Dishonesty in a marriage may be a power play or a symptom of guilty fear, or it could indicate an attitude of gender antagonism. Dishonesty is the enemy of intimacy, and destructive to marriage (Pittman 1989). Dishonesty coupled with guilt creates distance.

Romance in marriage often dies after the birth of children, when parents get involved in parenting and in making ends meet. Routine takes over and soon the importance of partners spending time with each other diminishes. When no attention is paid to the relationship, it gets worse. At times this has to do with how the partners grew up in their family of origin, where they had perhaps witnessed the same behaviors between their parents. As Gray (1992) indicates, from 40 to 70 percent of married couples are not satisfied with their partners and have had outside affairs. Some couples who stick it out are not even able to look at their problems and admit to themselves or to their partner that they are not satisfied. They keep up the appearance of a relationship when they are dying inside. It is often the loneliest place in the world, lying next to someone who doesn't love you anymore, or someone you have stopped loving. In another scenario, we often think our friends have a great marriage but suddenly hear they are getting a divorce; on the surface the marriage looked all right, but love must have died a long time ago.

When there is pain in a relationship, some people avoid looking for options. They try to justify the problems and tell themselves there is no such thing as a perfect relationship, and to expect more in a marriage is to be immature and unrealistic. Others who are disillusioned with their marriage move on to another. As they do not face their issues, they create the same scenario; then comes the second divorce because they have not worked through the original issues and thus face the same problems over and over again. These people may go from partner to partner avoiding self-examination. Still others may think it is too scary to risk leaving a relationship, and just give up. Many children watch their parents not being in love and hurting each other and talking about each other behind their backs. At times couples say that they love their partner but are not "in love." The popular belief is that romantic love does not last long; the truth is that real love does, and to make it grow it has to be nurtured and protected zealously.

Generally, people have learned about love and relationships by watching how their parents treat each other. Gray (1992) agrees with Lerner (1989) that most of the education about marriage occurs while growing up at home, particularly when you are very young and what you see has an unconscious influence on you. If children saw their parents lying to each other, they learned to lie. If they saw their parents hiding their real feelings, they learned to hide their own. If they saw parents punishing each other, they did the same in their own relationships. People are trained how to behave when they are very young, and they simultaneously learn about intimacy. Imitating their own parents, and not working on the relationship, leads to frustration and anger, which becomes coupled with guilt when they begin to have serious fantasies about leaving the relationship or having an affair.

People are uncannily efficient in choosing partners who will help them get into situations that will re-create earlier dilemmas that they have never mastered successfully.

Lincoln said, "There are elements of my mother's personality in Cecilia. She will run out on me and be flighty." But the earlier frustrating relationship with his adoptive mother was replicated in the present frustrating situation with his wife. He could not be in any other kind of marital relationship for this was the only kind he really knew about—one in which he felt dependent for nurturance (like his father) on a person for whom he had no real affectionate or loving feelings. Thus intimacy gets shortchanged.

SUBJECTIVE TRUTH

A person who has an affair and his or her partner face different types of truths. The person who is not having the affair is usually involved in family life, doing what is required, but perhaps not paying much attention to the physical needs of the couple. The person who is having the affair is upset at the home situation, but does not communicate and is unhappy about real or imagined wrong-doings. This individual has a need for attention but will not discuss it with his or her spouse.

> Drew had an affair with his secretary, April, after twenty-one years of being married to Winter. He found April pleasant, attractive, always well dressed, and ready to fulfill his every desire in the office. Her willingness to do his official work well led to more intimate conversations, and finally to an affair. When Winter found out, she was devastated. Drew accused her of not caring for him and not doing anything for him, such as dressing up for him or being passionate in their relationship. Winter tearfully repeated this in therapy, saying that he was not aware of how she is making a home for them and that she forgot through the years to do little things like dress up and go out for dinner. Everything at home was mundane, but there were four children who needed to be taken care of, and she was "doing everything to be a good mother." She added angrily, "If I dressed up and took care of all your office work then I would be a secretary too, and her job entails that she be pleasant and look out for you professionally because that is her job and she is getting paid for it." Drew was confused and angry that he had been found out, and was defensive about his behavior, but added that he wanted to work at the marriage. Blaming, retorts, and recounting of obligations and commitments ensued. However, blaming does not set anything right, but creates more problems.
>
> After the initial blow-out of angry fuses the couple settled down to discuss their issues. There were

constant surprises for each other. Often Winter would say that she did not know that her husband felt the way he did. She thought the marriage was doing fine. Drew complained that he felt unloved and unwanted, and added that it had been three months since he had sexual intercourse with his wife and that was long before he had the affair with April. He said that she was always in bed when he came home and he had to warm up his own dinner. She always complained that she was tired because she was looking after the children. He felt she was only a mother. Winter had been blissfully unaware of the affair but was surprised that he "did not bother about sex" in bed and felt relieved that he was not interested. She saw him as a good husband who took care of his own dinner, and she was not concerned when he began to spend a couple of hours in front of the TV before coming to bed. He would be in bed at midnight or later and Winter saw nothing wrong with it. However, with the affair she woke up and realized that he had been irritable with her quite a few times, but she had seen this as a result of tension in his workplace. The happy ending to this case was that both of them were willing to put forth the effort to work through the problems in their marriage.

Subjective truth also has to do with what each person has experienced in the family of origin. If parents quarreled constantly or did not communicate with each other, the children watched and learned similar ways to deal with their own problems. Even in ideal relationships, as Lerner (1989) indicates, there is some degree of reactive fighting and distancing.

> Andy would distance himself after a misunderstanding, but Lucy really wanted to discuss what brought about the misunderstanding. Andy would disappear into his study and return after a couple of hours, acting as if everything was perfectly all right, when it was not. In this fashion he developed *distance* in the marriage. Lucy accepted the distancing, thinking it was how he coped and adapted to issues, and if it felt comfortable for him, she would go along. She agonized over the issues that were never completely discussed or worked through. As she said in therapy, "I was tired of pursuing him and asking him questions about everything when he seemed so reluctant to communicate, so I gave up and thought that once we fought he would let it pass." He did not; he let it build up within him and distanced himself from his wife. He thought, and was angry, that she was putting him down and resented her as being critical, but would not communicate about it. She on the other hand saw him as being "all right" and did not know she was dealing with a boiling pot with a tight lid. She devoted her time to pleasing her boss and he devoted himself to his colleague, a beautiful single woman who encouraged him to discuss his marital problems, which eventually led them to have an affair.

Thus, extreme distancing and avoidance of discussions can lead to serious problems. Each of us lives with his or her subjective truth and the family patterns learned in our family of origin. When couples build a marriage, they need to look at their individual patterns and develop new patterns of behavior that are conducive to their marriage. This does not happen unless a great deal of effort is put into it. When there is a crisis such as infidelity, the couple may break up because the pain and lack of trust overwhelm them, but breaking up (as mentioned earlier) can often lead them to create similar relationships with others. Working through their issues and understanding each other can provide insight and better coping and adapting capabilities.

LOSS

At times life situations create problems that cannot be overlooked.

> When Margaret's grandmother died, it raised uncomfortable issues for Margaret, including concern for her mother's emotional well-being. It also brought back strong feelings about her earlier loss of her father. This led Margaret to distance herself from her family of origin. In treatment Margaret learned that distancing was by no means a protection from strong emotional reactions to deaths in the family and the unresolved grief that prevented her from creating meaningful relationships for herself, at work, or in her social life.

Sometimes the intense anxiety that fuels a current relationship problem may stem from an experience long past, such as incest, an early loss, or any number of "hot issues" that were swept under the rug in the family of origin. At times it may be relatively easy to make connections. "I know my problem of not being intimate with Sam has something to do with my history of sexual abuse." At other times there may be near-total amnesia.

> Stephanie and her sister Cathy were both in their forties, and had barely talked to each other since

their mother's death six years before. Cathy was still furious at Stephanie for not doing enough for their mother at the time of her greatest need; Stephanie believed that Cathy made unilateral decisions about their mother's care without consulting her. The siblings were locked in a mutual blaming stance that was heading toward total cutoff. Each saw the problem as the other's fault. Neither of them was aware that the intensity of their relationship, which was first managed by fighting and now by distancing, had as its source the high level of anxiety surrounding their mother's terminal illness and death. Staying angry and distant protected both Cathy and Stephanie from the full experience of their grief, which they would be better able to meet head-on if they truly reconciled and drew together.

Losses, when not handled well, include anger and grief; this is carried over to other relationships. People often move from one relationship to another without working out their grief and re-create situations so the same problems arise again and again. Because of the carryover of grief they are stifled in their new relationship, and the warmth and caring prevalent during the dating days quickly disappears in marriage. The old grief and its unresolved issues become part of the marital relationship. The person falls back into the old patterns and has expectations that are carried over from earlier unresolved pain and other issues. This creates problems for both of them that, if not resolved, can lead to divorce—and the pattern of dating and remarriage starts again. There is pain and anger at the end of the relationship, but the person never stops for self-examination. Often such people are superficial and pretend a great deal, using cliches to present their point of view and opinion. They may even appear to be flamboyant and happy, but much of their behavior is a put-on that quickly disappears under stress.

Losses make people distance themselves from significant others or act as if they do not need people. When trouble arises in an intimate relationship and people ignore it, do not put out any new energy, or look at new options for change, the problems are likely to escalate. However, it is never too late to learn to move differently in our key relationships. In the short run, the changes that people make and the initial reactions may leave a person feeling scared, frustrated, angry or very separate. But like many things in life, it becomes a matter of sitting with short-term anxiety for long-term gain (Lerner 1989).

SENSE OF VICTIMIZATION

People who are not acknowledged for what they do and how they function are likely to experience victimization. When growing up, some children are told they have to be perfect, not to create waves, listen to parents, and do only what the parents want them to do. The children experience victimization but are not aware of it. Often their identities are foreclosed and the children carry on the work their parents want them to do, not questioning the justice or the wisdom of what is happening. They comply with other people's wishes and act as their parents wish—like perfect children. They undermine or deny their own needs and desires and overreflect and overwork at the needs of their parents. They do not discuss controversial topics at home. A fight between parents is called an "argument," no matter how angry and violent the fighting has been or how long it has gone on. There is no sense of intimacy in the family and the children turn out to be puppets doing what is required of them by the parents. They see their parents as omniscient, omnipotent, and almost "perfect" despite the underlying feelings of hostility they may detect. Such children learn to deny their own feelings just as their parents do. Their sense of intimacy is warped at an early age. They learn to deny their true feelings, and are always ready to please others and overlook their own welfare for the well-being of others. Such people function well in positive situations, but fail terribly when faced with negative situations. They do not develop the inner strength to be what or who they should be.

As Lerner (1989) so vividly puts it, from the time children are wrapped in their first blankets they are encouraged to express certain traits, qualities, or behaviors and to deny or inhibit others. Throughout our lives we also learn that the survival of our relationships and the very integrity of our family depend upon our being and functioning in a particular way. In a similar fashion we also send out communications about our expectations to others. Learning what others want and expect from us helps to make us civilized human beings.

All family systems develop around a set of shared beliefs and stances that are conveyed to each member. Family stances are beliefs about mottoes, attitudes, and behavior, including communication patterns. Children are taught communication styles as infants, long before they understand words. The family's communication style includes tolerance of conflict, the need for agreement, or the ability to be emotionally honest. People may learn to block their feelings about their family because of the need to protect themselves or other family members from being hurt.

Areas profoundly influenced by family attitudes are

self-esteem, independence, and initiative. There are children who come from toxic families who need parental approval for everything, which prevents them from making their own decisions in important areas of life. As Forward (1989) indicates, all adults have at least some ongoing enmeshment with their parents. One question that might be asked of such people is, "Can you have your thoughts, actions, and feelings and not place into them your parents' hopes, expectations, behaviors, needs, or desires?" Only a few can answer with a categorical "no." Many are defensive about their answers but it is important to understand that physically moving away from home does not necessarily entail emotional growth.

> Candy said in therapy, "I'm embarrassed, but I guess I was living up to my parents' expectations of being the bright one who can handle anything. Although I failed in my marriages, they still think I can do it all. Besides, I'm still at their beck and call, doing for them things they can do for themselves." As an afterthought she added, "I run home seventy miles to take my mother to the doctor when she can drive herself, or my sister, who lives three blocks away, can do it. When my marriage broke up for the third time, my mother pretended that nothing happened and that I was a fine, bright person. What does brightness have to do with my emotions? I'm ashamed that I'm so tied to my parents and they can pull the strings any way they want and I move in that direction. I realize that problems in my marriages also had to do with my parents always wanting me to do things for them and their inability to understand that I needed to spend time with my husband. They always grumbled that my husbands were very selfish and couldn't think of my own poor parents." Candy real-

ized that even as an adult she was still being controlled by her parents, and her sense of victimization overwhelmed her when she thought of the failures that became part of her life. She lost custody of her child because her lawyer husband was able to prove that she was overextended and would not be an effective parent. Her second husband turned to other women, and her last husband walked out on her when she chose to spend her birthday with her parents rather than with him. As an afterthought, with a great deal of shame, she added that she had also spent Thanksgiving and Christmas with them. When her husband refused to accompany her, she went by herself and her parents put down her husband, saying she was too good for him.

Candy finally understood that she had to break the bonds of enmeshment in order to begin her own life. She was very angry at her own discoveries. Although at first she was impulsive and wanted to challenge her parents, she realized that they might not change and the first step she had to make was to take charge of her life. Sometime during her upbringing she learned that it was not all right to desire for herself, to appreciate herself, or to express herself, but this could change by processing the destructive bonds that tied her so deeply to her family of origin.

CHALLENGING ONE'S BELIEFS

As children, we learn about ourselves and our parents. Our beliefs are deeply ingrained in our attitudes, perceptions, and concepts about people, relationships, and morality. Those who make repetitive mistakes in relationships and find themselves in toxic or hurtful situations need to ask themselves why this happens. In order to change, they must look at the erroneous beliefs, negative feelings, and self-defeating behaviors that have been ingrained from childhood.

When adults who have grown up complying with their parents' wishes all their lives want to challenge their parents, they often feel helpless. Their belief works like this: "I cannot win, although I feel mistreated, because my parents have all the power." When people think someone else has the all the power, they continue to feel helpless, afraid, frustrated, and overwhelmed. To defend themselves against these enmeshed feelings, people may back down automatically and give in to their parents' wishes (Forward 1989). As Gray (1984) indicates, repressing feelings is actually a safety mechanism that people have developed through the years. When they are unable to cope with and express their emotions, they learn to hide those feelings deep inside, hoping they will just go away. Through many years of rejecting and suppressing their own emotions, they acquire the unfortunate and unhealthy habit of automatically repressing any unsafe, unacceptable, or confusing emotion. They learn to express only those feelings that won't disturb or threaten their lives, thereby ensuring safety and acceptance. They become strangers to their own feelings. They figure out in their heads what to feel, rather than simply and spontaneously feeling from the heart. People who are very enmeshed, who do not know how to deal with their issues, frequently use drugs or alcohol in an attempt to avoid all feelings.

As Forward (1989) indicates, and as I have seen with my own clients, there are people who say:

> "It is up to me to make my parents happy."
> "I am my parents' whole life."

"My parents' feelings are more important than mine."
"There is no point in talking to my parents because it wouldn't do any good."
"No matter what they did, they are my parents and I have to honor them." (As an 11-year-old said, "I must love my mother even if she hurts me, because I came out of her stomach!")
At an angry extreme: "My parents do not have any control over my life. I fight with them all the time."

Conversely, there *are* individuals who continue to fight the images of their parents long after they have left home. They too might be seen as tied to their parents, because their emotional energy is being used to rebel against their parents rather than setting and moving toward their own goals.

Lynn, the second daughter in the family, married a man of a different faith when she was almost 30 years old. Her mother encouraged her to get married because "that was the only way to live—with a man." Lynn obediently obliged. The older daughter, Martha, had moved away from home and barely kept in touch with her parents. Lynn was the "baby," and her mother made sure this daughter would do right by her. She did not mind that the boyfriend, Frank, belonged to a different faith. Lynn considered herself fortunate because Frank was kind, caring, and understanding. When Lynn came home from work, he would have dinner hot and ready. When she wanted to take a bath, he would run the water for her, and she was thrilled. They had a beautiful wedding and Lynn's mother was overjoyed. Her new son-in-law had a master's degree in chemical engineering and was making good money. The mother, who was ambitious for Lynn, told her daughter that Frank had to get his doctorate and at the same time provide for her. She asked Lynn to help Frank understand that a doctorate would provide better for them. She encouraged Lynn to give up her job and stay home so she could have a baby. Lynn, who had spent all her adult life trying to win her mother's approval, followed her mother's advice and gave up her job. Then she started to pressure her husband to get his doctorate. Although he was hesitant as he had just completed his master's, he began taking courses at the local university. He began to feel overwhelmed; he was working full-time, was newly married and in a new, more expensive apartment, and was a doctoral student. At her mother's insistence, Lynn began to take things easy; lying in bed until noon because she had to be "relaxed" to get pregnant, and slowly overlooking the housework. When Frank came home, he cooked and cleaned while Lynn complained about not becoming pregnant. Within eight months they divorced. Lynn went back to live with her parents until she could get a job and get back on her feet. A job made Lynn more independent economically and she went into therapy. In therapy she learned that her relationship with her parents, particularly her mother, was toxic, and that her mother had control over Lynn's desires and feelings. This led to anger and pain. Lynn left the therapist because her mother informed her that "the therapist was screwed up." On and on this went: Lynn would find the ideal therapist but the mother insisted on knowing what was happening in the sessions and would sabotage the therapy. No one was good enough to help her daughter, because the mother herself was a "therapist" who worked in a local agency. Ten years passed while Lynn shopped around for therapists and found no one good enough. She gave up her promising position as a manager in a company and became a salesperson. By this time her anger had turned against her mother and she fought her all the time. Finally, a friend Lynn called at odd times of the night to talk about her problems got tired of it and recommended yet another therapist.

Lynn was in therapy with me for one year. One of her biggest fears at this time was that her mother would interfere in and sabotage any relationship she created with a man, and she desperately wanted to get married. One of my biggest challenges was to help her change her habitual patterns of behavior: calling her mother frequently, or allowing her mother to call her. (The mother always asked her if she had met anyone yet.) Lynn, in her early forties, still saw herself as a victim, and also felt unconsciously that she had to "make her mother happy" and "always be a good daughter," although she had begun to fight back when the mother gave Lynn her opinions. Guilt overwhelmed Lynn if she did not communicate everything to her mother, but she consciously worked at creating distance between herself and her mother, and systematically and diligently learned to look at her own needs and desires.

CHANGING HABITUAL PATTERNS

Adult children who have been abused must realize that they are not obligated to their parents for everything. Lynn had to learn in therapy that it was neither cruel nor hurtful to stop accepting responsibility for her mother's happiness. It was up to the mother, who had a job and a husband, to make herself find ways to feel better. Lynn learned in therapy to tell her mother, "I'm sorry, but I don't want to share information about my dating life with you," and when her mother became manipulative, to add, "I'm sorry you're upset." Lynn had to learn that it was not her responsibility to change her life to suit her mother, or change her plans for the sole purpose of pleasing her mother. One of Lynn's greatest problems was her belief that she was somehow responsible for taking care of her mother's feelings. However, when she ignored her own needs for the sake of her mother, she built up anger and resentment that affected all her relationships, particularly those with men. Lynn realized that she had not been successful in making her mother happy in all these years, and might never do so. This made her feel guilty and inadequate about herself.

As Forward (1989) indicates, if you base most of your life decisions on how they will make your parents feel, you relinquish free choice. When their feelings always come first, your parents will be in the driver's seat for the rest of your life.

Lynn tried to figure out all the negative beliefs she was brought up with that kept her from being an effective adult with her parents.

Even during therapy, when Lynn had a date she called her mother and they talked about it. It was easy for me to make Lynn aware of her behaviors, but it was up to Lynn to make the *changes*. After Lynn understood the self-defeating beliefs that made her feel awful, she moved on to change her behaviors, though it was difficult for her to turn off her emotional faucets. She had been told as a child that her mother was all-wise and all-powerful, and she got the strong message that it was not "nice" to judge your mother. She remembered once asking her mother why she was beating her older sister for what seemed like a trivial reason, such as not cleaning the dishes properly. Lynn, the mother's favorite child, asked the question because she was horrified by the severity of the sister's beating. The mother cried and complained to Lynn's uncle about her younger daughter's behavior. After the uncle belted the younger girl a couple of times for being bad, Lynn was forced to face the wall for over an hour. From that time on Lynn was too scared to question her mother or talk to her father about anything as he was too distant. She was made to feel distant and scared of him by the mother, who would tell her, "He's in a rotten mood, don't disturb him. He won't be of any help to you." This information was deeply buried in Lynn and she was not in touch with all the pain she had accumulated from her parents. In her relationships with men she acted out her family's dance by shutting down when important matters needed to be discussed, at the same time wanting to please her mother and always be the favorite child.

Lynn had to learn to fully experience her emotions and express the complete truth about them. Releasing her emotions did not mean dumping them on anyone indiscriminately; rather, she had to be selective, perhaps with a therapist. At times, telling the complete truth is the only hope. Instead of pretending everything is fine, admitting that you made a mistake is important, far better than spending the rest of your life blaming someone. Therapy begins with sharing your hurt and sadness and having the willingness to change.

Personal and family problems repeat themselves in patterns. They come back, signaling their presence through discomfort and pain. Perhaps your spouse betrayed you or your teenager stayed out past curfew. If people do not figure out the underlying causes of these problems, they will probably happen again, but with new characters and/or in new ways.

Family patterns are created because people are likely

to do what is familiar, even when things are not working smoothly. The person does not realize there may be other ways of doing it. The root of the old ways of doing things goes back to his or her family experiences from childhood and adolescence. We can never really divorce ourselves from our families of origin. Foster (1993) uses the term *family's life stance*, which means that every family has a shared approach to daily life through attitudes and behavior. People can explore how their family met the challenges of daily life, with optimism or pessimism, actively or passively. If the family had a destructive life stance, such as frozenness or flatness, a lack of interest and energy; if there were anxiety, doubts, or fears that life is dangerous and resources are scarce; if there were limitations or helplessness, that is, tunnel vision that cannot conceive of hopeful possibilities; or if there was rigidity, that is, control and unwillingness to alter the status quo, then many problems can result.

> Miranda was the divorced mother of Anna, 11, and Maureen, 9. Her first marriage broke up some six years before and her former husband was no longer in contact with them. Miranda relied on her close, large family for childcare and support. Later she invited Rich, a mechanic she dated for three years, to move in with them. Miranda's children liked Rich but he often felt like an outsider, and wished the extended family weren't so ever-present. Miranda's motto with her family had always been "You and me against the world." Rich wanted her to form a new family with him; each of them said that their biggest problem was communication.

Many people who suffer from lack of intimacy as adults do so because their first relationship taught them that the world is a cruel and unsafe place, and that they should not trust anybody or anything. When mistrust overwhelms them, they believe that life is unfair, and that they are unworthy and incompetent. Some people more or less "adjust" to living within this "wall of mistrust."

In other cases, however, the repetitive problems become too painful. When the individuals cannot take it anymore, they decide to do something about it and bring about change in themselves. Changing habitual patterns is a cyclic process. It involves becoming aware of what the problem is and gathering information on what is going on, tracing the current problems from their roots in the family pattern, and assessing change in terms of how it affects you and others in your life. People can plan for and create changes, and so the cycle begins. A person then has to reassess the situation and alter the plan of action until the problem is solved. Increasing awareness will not necessarily change painful situations unless action is taken.

The influences of family patterns are subtle and complex, and touch all aspects of a person's life in deep and hidden ways. Just like a computer, the mind holds in its memory a wealth of information that can help people understand their family patterns. When family structures are revealed, family patterns can be recognized and understood.

> When Eva was writing about her mother's influence, she systematically teased out the different ways she was influenced by her mother. She took care of her younger siblings as well as the other people at home and at work. As a young person, when she complained, her mother lashed out at her and her father became depressed. So Eva did everything to please her parents. In her workplace she was helpful to everyone

> and felt overstretched. She did not know how to say "no" to her boss, who overwhelmed her with his demands. In therapy, Eva mentioned insightfully that her boss was not her parent and she should begin to set limits. She began to write about herself, and to assess and explore her options, and to respond creatively rather than automatically.

Changing behavior patterns takes time, effort, and energy. All persons in a family are interconnected. Something that touches one person affects the whole system. Because family patterns carry such weight, family members must identify the *themes* that run through the family. By tracing a problem to its roots in your present life, you can observe how you repeat the past; with that knowledge you are more equipped to make life-affirming changes. The common theme that Eva found in her family and in herself was the desire to please others, and underneath it all "each one of us was plainly trying to get noticed and be loved."

While trying to make changes in family-based patterns, a person has to go slowly, take small steps, expect resistances and surprises, and remember that change is a process, not a product. We refer to the process as cyclic because of the need for continuous reassessment of the situation.

One of the important things people have to do in dealing with relationship problems is to restructure their boundaries, that is, change the rules, beliefs, and feelings about how people relate to others. A person has to view himself or herself as being separate from others and must develop his or her own sense of self. Boundaries give and withhold permission for others to enter our personal space, both emotionally and physically. Healthy boundaries can be learned through social interaction, direct teaching, and modeling. The person has to make a contract for change by admitting that there was a violation of boundaries, such as "I was abused," or "I had to take care of the family in terms of responsibilities and work." After recognizing and admitting a pattern, a person has to get in touch with how he or she felt at that time and feels now. *Connection* with the patterns is important. Eva said, "When I did a great deal of work, I was still seen as not being good enough, which means that at a later point I would try even harder to make people like me." At times, when people get in touch with their feelings, they are also mourning the loss of the sense of self-esteem, loss of meaningful relationships, and pain over the losses. They have to think through the important part of their life that needs boundary repair. A person who has not had healthy boundaries really does not know what it is to have them. Therefore, the person has to imagine specific changes, and how people would react to them. If someone said something to you that sounded like a put-down, would you still be a people-pleaser? Or would you clarify, communicate, and enforce your own boundaries? If you do not want to do something for the parents who still exploit you, how would you deal with such a situation? Can you say something like, "I have something else to do right now," rather than running to please them? A therapist, friend, relative, or colleague can help you make yourself accountable for how you create and maintain healthy new boundaries. Constant, conscious efforts are needed to change old habits into new and healthy ones. It is easy to fall back into unhealthy patterns when there is stress and uncertainty, but it is important to recognize the fall and move back to the new level you have created for yourself. Encouragement and support, coupled with persistence, can lead people to move to higher levels. When a person persistently works on changing and redefining personal boundaries in a healthy manner, changes happen.

AUTONOMY AND CHOICE

When boundaries become clear, the satisfying experience of personal choice is possible. As Beavers (1985) indicates, many apparently healthy people have never experienced the satisfaction of individual choice in any significant area of life. Every decision they make is ascribed to authority, relatives, spouses, or children; in this way an unholy bargain is made and the balance is maintained. This also means that "things were done to me and I'm not responsible for anything," and "I have no control over my life and therefore I am blameless."

Such people always blame others for the things that have gone wrong in their lives. To place blame appropriately is useful when pointing out problems and reactions to them, but it becomes unhealthy if done all the time. For instance, when there is tension between a husband and wife, or a father and son, there doesn't have to be a continually frustrating oppositional struggle. Through boundary-making, a person learns to make decisions, to commit to ideas, roles, activities, and people. A person is known by his or her choices and commitments; this expresses personhood. Families vary in competence in their ability to resolve ambivalence and to make choices.

> Antonia continued to pressure her only son to become a medical doctor. Edward was opposed to the idea, but wavered constantly. His ambivalence gave his mother more power. Once he had resolved the issue in his own mind, the conflict moved to an interpersonal arena, and conflict resolutions became the family's responsibility. This became pos-

> sible only because Edward took responsibility for his feelings and choices, and when he made up his mind he told his mother and other family members what he wanted to do. His firmness resolved the family conflict effectively. With adequate reasons and constructive discussions, Edward chose to become a physicist, and the entire family helped Antonia understand the need for her support and encouragement.

For family members to function effectively in families, they must move in a coherent manner toward resolving ambivalence. Positive relationships between family members are crucial, not only for the family unit but for the growth and development of the individuals in the family. The individual and the family are not at odds, but depend upon each other. Family systems do not change automatically, as Beavers (1985) indicates, but family members, at times with the help of therapists, change the system. The ability to communicate—to work at relationships, to confront comfortably and still be loved—depends on the degree of intimacy present in the family.

As this book illustrates, there are varying degrees of intimacy; feeling intimate means being able to communicate about what you really feel and think. When intimacy in a relationship fails, for example, a person is filled with stress, and his or her mind works in two different ways: (1) seeing the whole picture, which may be overwhelming, and (2) looking at the pieces that make up the whole.

To work through a conflict or problem, one must look at his or her emotions, broaden his or her perspective, and apply insight for problem solving. While developing intimacy, a person has to pay careful attention to boundaries of self and others, and really put effort and time into building both the boundaries and the bridges. One of the chief ingredients of intimacy is trust. Without it one cannot feel real or intimate.

There are different levels of intimacy. A child who confides his or her wishes to a parent hopes that the wishes will be respected. How does a child who has been sexually, physically, or emotionally abused learn to be intimate with anyone in the family of origin or in adult relationships? It is a long, slow, painful, and risky process, but it can and will happen. The intimacy a person develops in present-life relationships can heal, or at least diminish, the demons of the past by risking vulnerability with healthy people. At times, couples come into therapy with paranoid mistrust. This happens when there are more and more problems that seem to overwhelm the couples' marriage.

> Jeff was extremely mistrustful of his wife, Judy, but he also believed in being trustworthy to her, meaning not letting a loved person down. Judy had a similar way of looking at trust, but she objected to Jeff's attacks, although she believed that he was justified because she had been unfaithful more than once. Her current lack of interest added to his suspicions, which indicated to the therapist that there was, for him, no reservoir of trust. Jeff frequently called Judy's office, followed every move she made, and questioned her in great detail if she was even a few minutes late. In turn, she called him a nag and would slip away to do something harmless, like spend time in a shopping mall. Because he had been betrayed a few times, he painfully awaited her arrival at home to start a fight about where she had been.

How could you develop trust in such a situation? Beavers (1985) says, "Help others not to hurt you," particularly when there is awareness of ambivalence and therefore awareness of relative trust. Fortunately, Judy was able to respond to her husband's rage and depression with kindness, signifying to the therapist that she had a reservoir of trust upon which to build. According to Ellis (1977), in situations like this case, the intimacy patterns of the family of origin and past relationships have to be examined. Doing things together, bonding, and closeness are not the same as intimacy. Intimacy, as discussed earlier, entails being vulnerable and mutually self-disclosing. Was talking openly a shameful matter in your family of origin? Were you made to feel shame because you were honest? If your family did not satisfy your needs for intimacy, where did you seek it and with whom? To develop an intimate relationship you have to be able to trust another person—who would this person be? Intimacy is elusive: the more one presses for it, the less it can occur. It requires trust and willingness, which can be earned only through time as a relationship progresses. In developing intimacy we learn to trust, through a process of trial and error that teaches us how much to open up, what areas are safe to share, and whether confidence will be respected. A person also needs to learn communication skills, which is the work of relationships. In constructive communication there is willingness to think through one's thoughts and feelings and to share them with another. Besides sharing, it is important to listen. According to Ellis's (1977) research, we spend about 45 percent of our time listening and only 30 percent of the time speaking, and many people are bad listeners. Good listening is more than interaction of the ear; it is the ability to respond in ways that reflect understanding and encourage further disclosure. In listening, we need to become communication enhancers, which does not include advising, correcting, judging, or deflecting another person's feelings. To be good listeners, people have to get in touch with their own feelings. A balance must be created between listening and sharing, between being too passive and being too domineering. Risking self-disclosure is the door we have to pass through to obtain intimacy. However, throughout the process people have to pay attention to their own boundaries, which are the dividing lines between individuals. Some people seem to have no boundaries at all. They repeatedly allow themselves to be used and abused, and tell their story, with no sense of privacy or shame, to anyone who will listen. At the other extreme are people whose boundaries seem impenetrable. We may know them for years, but do not really *know* them, because they do not share their thoughts or feelings. In between are people whose boundaries are clear but permeable. They preserve their sense of self, their right to privacy, but can also enter into and maintain intimate relationships in which there is considerable sharing, self-disclosure, and mutual concern.

How can clients be helped to reach a point where they experience clear boundaries and a positive sense of self in relationships? In the following two cases boundary-making and development of trust and intimacy happened through therapy. In one case the client had no boundaries for setting limits or separating herself from the problems of other family members; in the second case the client had very rigid boundaries, to the point of excluding and alienating anyone who came too close to him.

Case #1

Ruth was introduced to me as an emergency case while I was at the university working on a speech. The intake worker from the agency called me out of desperation, saying that my new client, whom I had not seen in person, was in crisis and needed to speak to me. Although I am usually skeptical of such emergencies, something in the intake worker's voice made me pick up the phone. On the other end I heard the tremulous voice of my client. She needed to see me immediately, she said. I asked what was bothering her; could she explain her situation? The client, Ruth, panicked, began to cry, saying that she was overwhelmed, and that her medication did not help her much at this point. Both her sons had been suspended from school for bad behavior, she lamented, and the boss at her workplace, a small fast-food restaurant, was getting impatient because every so often she had to leave work to pick up the boys. In the same breath she added that she had to take her sick mother to the doctor as she would not drive herself, even though his office was nearby, and that her husband would be mad if dinner was not ready on time. I told her I experienced her as being overwhelmed, and suggested that she didn't have to do everything that very minute. I asked why her husband could not pick up the sons; she did not have an answer. She had never asked him, she said, and similarly had never asked her mother to drive herself to the doctor's. As I made the suggestions, Ruth calmed down. I continued to be supportive, and asked her to meet me at the appointed time in my office the next day. Quietly, Ruth agreed.

Ruth was a 40-year-old woman with unkempt hair who dressed carelessly in white pants and a loose blouse. As we proceeded in therapy, it was clear that she had grown up in a home where there was no intimacy. Her father was an alcoholic and her mother a nurse who worked into the night. Ruth at age 8 took care of her older brother, who was 10, as well as her father. She cooked and cleaned after school, and felt like a "little adult" all her life. At the age of 9 she was sexually abused by her father; this abuse continued until she was 13. She was the father's "princess" and her brother was the "bad kid" who was severely beaten, for "no good reason," whenever the father was drunk. Ruth hated her father. When her mother was home, there were constant arguments and fights between the mother and father, and Ruth, in her role as peacemaker, afraid for her parents' marriage, did not tell her mother about the sexual abuse until, at age 13, she could not hide her shame, guilt, and pain and told her mother. After a series of fights that lasted a number of days, the mother threw the father out of the house. Since then, the mother had acted as if nothing had happened. There was no discussion of the abuse or any sympathy for Ruth. Ruth began to feel guilty about her parents' separation and felt doubly committed to doing all the housework. Occasionally her father came by the house, totally drunk, and threatened his wife, as he wanted to live with them. One day when he came home with a knife, Ruth's mother called the police and he was arrested. After that incident Ruth saw him only once or twice. Again there was no discussion of the family problems. Ruth left home when she was 18 and got married. Her father, she heard, died shortly after that. Ruth's brother, who was more like her son, died in a swimming accident. Ruth's mother remarried twice; both her husbands died, one in an accident and the second after a bout with ill health. The mother moved to a house near Ruth. By this time Ruth was the mother of three sons, aged 19, 13, and 11. She described her husband,

Willy, as very demanding and abusive to the children. The father threw Marcus, the oldest son, out of the house after a physical fight. The son never returned home to live, and did not complete high school. Marcus lived with a young woman and had a daughter. He was unemployed off and on and Ruth secretly provided for him.

Willy had been an active alcoholic but had given up drinking two years earlier. He was better with her and did not mistreat the children; he had never mistreated Ruth. He was a computer buff and spent every hour at home after work in front of the computer. Throughout her talk, Ruth appeared to be angry with her husband for not being a good father.

An intergenerational pattern between Ruth's father and the husband began to be evident. Willy did not participate in housework but expected the house to look clean at all times. He did not approve of her sons "making noise," which meant watching television.

When I asked Ruth, "How do you feel about your father?" it looked as if her whole world came tumbling down. Clearly in torment, and with a torrent of tears, she screamed that she was glad he was dead. She had spat on his grave because he was "a son of a bitch." Ruth's mother had taken no responsibility for what happened to Ruth as a child. She added that her mother always made her feel guilty about the abuse, as if Ruth had deliberately taken part in it. Her mother used guilt to control Ruth, and to get her to run all her errands for her. Ruth had been in therapy a couple of times before seeing me, and the mother sabotaged the sessions by questioning the content of the sessions and then putting down the therapist. The mother also told Ruth that Willy was "a lousy husband."

After a few sessions I suggested a family session. Ruth agreed. Her husband did not come but the two younger sons did. In this session the strong alliance between the two sons and the mother was obvious. From the outside this looked like a family with two working parents and a couple of children, but there was so much pent-up anger in Ruth that it flowed freely all over the session. While she was putting down her husband, she would anxiously look at the sons for approval, but they sat with heads bowed, staring at the floor. She cajoled them, seeking their support: "Aren't I right? Isn't it true that all three of us have problems with him, and he's not at all understanding?"

Self-consciously, the sons nodded their heads. At one point, however, the 13-year-old, Murphy, protested; the younger brother, Bruno, nodded in agreement without lifting his head. Murphy looked at his mother and stated, "Dad's not that bad." At this juncture I pointed out the alliance between Ruth and the boys against the husband. My comment surprised Ruth, who presented herself as an all-giving martyr. Abruptly she said: "Am I a bad person? And is he the good person?" "No," I answered, and then added slowly, "Ruth, this is not a war. It's your family, and you and your husband could be good people." She agreed, and with a great deal of guilt added, "What's wrong with me? I always feel I have to fight him." I asked, "Why don't you bring him for the next session?" Overwhelmed, Ruth confessed that she had not even asked him to attend the current session. She began to cry, saying that she felt guilty and ashamed. Later, I deliberately and emphatically discussed her chaotic family background and her inability to create supportive, caring relationships.

This was followed by four sessions with Ruth and her husband, Willy. Surprisingly, Willy talked about his former alcoholism and how he had changed for the better. Shifting gears, he talked about his wife's overextending herself. "Ruth does *everything* for *everyone* in the family, as well as her work colleagues." He noted that she is always "running, picking up someone whose car broke down, or bringing home a colleague who had a rough day, but she cannot look out for herself." He added, "She will talk to the whole world, but won't talk to me about anything." Ruth jumped in: "I thought you weren't interested in the children." "They're my children, too, but they're always afraid of me," Willy responded in an accusatory manner, implying that the children had been set up against him. "You used to drink, and you beat up Marcus." Willy sighed. "That was four years ago, and I didn't just beat him up, he was beating on his younger brother and wouldn't stop, and you forgot, we had to take Murphy to the emergency room because his nose was broken." At a later point, he added, "You encouraged Marcus to leave home. He's a high-school dropout now." Ruth struggled with her tears. "I'm not a good wife and I'm not a good mother." Before I could intervene, Willy added, "No, you *are* a good mother and a good wife and a very good daughter. Your mother goes to the spa every evening, but you get her groceries for her and even carry food to her every other day." In spite of his initial anger with "her over-giving self," by the end of the second session it was clear that Willy loved his wife and wished to do his share to help in the household chores, as well as to help his children with their homework. He wanted his children to grow up well and be "better than me."

In my individual sessions with Ruth she became aware of the intimacy problems that rose from her past. After a number of sessions, she worked through her anger with her father. This included working through her fears, anxiety, and anger about her sexual relationship with her husband, and the guilt she attached to sex. We dealt with her subjective truth and loss of childhood; the sense of victimization, extreme guilt, and shame she had experienced with her father during the sexual abuse, in which she saw herself as a participant and not as a victim because she was not supported by her mother. Her mother actually used the sexual abuse against Ruth in subtle ways, implying that Ruth was responsible for it. The mother was actually a self-sufficient, thrice-married and widowed woman with property in her own name. Nevertheless, she used her daughter's guilt to control her. In therapy Ruth learned that she had been only a child and was not responsible for the sexual abuse that she had experienced. She was the victim.

In later sessions Ruth, through rituals such as talking to her father's photo and telling him about her feelings, and letter-writing, gradually cleansed herself of the guilt and shame. Willy, whom she mixed up with her father, was seen as a different person, a kind and caring human being who had been through his own ordeals of pain as he recovered from alcoholism. Ruth connected her attempts to keep her husband an outsider with the children, and the carryover of unresolved issues of her childhood, as she worked through a journal and discussed the issues with the therapist. As she began to recognize her patterns, I gave her task assignments. One of Ruth's biggest problems was her inability to be nice to herself. She saw herself as unworthy and would not buy things for herself. In therapy, after much initial resistance, she began to learn to nurture herself. Her initial and overt nurturing included the simple task of buying a sweater she had always wanted. After the early attempts to buying the sweater, Ruth would tell me, with tears in her eyes, that she did not feel worthy enough to buy herself anything.

As time passed, Ruth learned to nurture herself, to be real in her feelings with her spouse and children, including telling them what she needed from them for herself. She learned to hug and kiss her children, and tell them that she loved them, and to receive the same from them. Ruth and Willy learned to have relevant conversations with each other about positive and negative matters. More than anyone else, she surprised herself by her ability to discuss intimate sexual matters with her husband, and for the first time in her 41 years, she learned to wholeheartedly appreciate her marriage and her children. She learned to draw boundaries and value herself. With reference to her mother, Ruth refused to do things the mother could do for herself. At first, her mother was skeptical, and called her the "new Ruth" for a few weeks, but as Ruth maintained her boundaries and her time with her family, the mother backed away and refrained from asking questions about Ruth's therapy. In therapy Ruth learned to talk about matters that bothered her, including being overwhelmed by her co-workers' demands. She previously overextended herself to please everyone, but this also changed. She reported that once she said "no" when she did not feel like helping someone, she felt good, "like I was taking care of myself." Her boss, who had found her indispensable, stopped being overdemanding, and Ruth openly mentioned that she would not stay late to close the restaurant as it was not her responsibility, but would do it if she was given a raise. She got her raise.

This case, unlike some others, was successful as Ruth's growth as a person, as well as her abilities to set limits, was realized. She learned about intimacy, in which the vulnerability of each person was acknowledged in the family circle. Ruth moved on to greater self-confidence, maturity, and stability in her life. Much of this success was due to Ruth's readiness and ability to confront her own fears, the "demons in my head," her hurts, and her fear of intimacy, and move to a higher level of functioning with her family closely involved by their growth and understanding and acceptance of Ruth's growth and progress. Ruth learned about loving, valuing, and respecting herself, and about setting limits and creating boundaries with family members and co-workers. Her husband was helpful throughout. He moved from being a computer buff to participating in housework and in his sons' lives, and stopped feeling like an intruder.

I cannot close this discussion without mentioning how Ruth looked as time passed. An unkempt, anxious woman initially, I watched her learn to dress up, put her hair up, and look more sophisticated. Nobody could miss the glow in her face and her eyes.

Case #2

Eric was a different case; rigidity in personal boundaries and difficulties in intimacy were the key problems in his marriage. He was a professor who dated his own students. He had lived with a student for seven years, and they had moved together to a new area. One day he came home to find a note on the kitchen table from his girlfriend as she walked out of his life permanently, taking her belongings with her. Later he learned she had returned to her old hometown, because she had moved only reluctantly to the new town.

In the new area Eric became friendly with one of his older students, Michelle, and later her husband, Chet, and their two teenaged children. Michelle, an undergraduate student in her late thirties, aspired to be an intellectual like her professor. Her husband, Chet, a down-to-earth construction worker, enjoyed a good game of football and would rather watch a boxing match on television than participate in any form of intellectual discussion. Michelle was dissatisfied with her marriage and unburdened her problems on her professor–friend Eric. Michelle soon got divorced and married Eric. Eric, who had been supportive and understanding in their friendship, suddenly closed up. He became a stranger with dark moods and a temper, and was secretive and private. Michelle moved into his house and sold hers. They had a prenuptial agreement: Michelle had no rights to his house or any of his belongings. His house was paid for, and Michelle had to ask permission to decorate or move her own things around in the house. The only rooms she could redecorate minimally were the kitchen and her side of the bedroom. The living room and other rooms, including the bathroom, were out of bounds. Eric constantly informed Michelle that it was *his* house, and Michelle felt like a guest. Her older daughter was away at college, and the second teenage daughter, Suzi, and Eric had ugly verbal fights because she would not listen to his rules. One day he locked her out of the house. After this, and with Michelle's help, Suzi moved to her father's house.

Michelle found out that Eric did not really trust her. When she discovered him talking to someone on the phone, he would accuse her of being suspicious and shut the door on her. He had a number of women friends in whom he would confide or listen to their problems. He could be very understanding, and would stay on the phone for two hours or more. He would not talk with Michelle about his friendships or conversations.

Everything in the house was marked "his" or "hers." If Michelle by accident touched Eric's things, he would curse her. Often he would scold her as if she were a child, although they were actually close in age. Eric and Michelle were in individual therapy with two different therapists, and finally came to me as a couple.

Eric came from a family where "you shouldn't show your feelings . . . feelings were a weakness in people." With this upbringing, of course, intimacy was at a stalemate. Eric remembered being bitten by a dog as a child and taken to the hospital. He was hurt that neither parent showed any emotion. He was flabbergasted by their businesslike attitude in taking him to the hospital. Many years later, he heard his younger brother mention that his mother had been upset and had run to the bathroom, crying as she saw Eric bleeding from the dog bite; their father was yelling at her to control herself. In retrospect, Eric was pleased by this. He realized his mother cared, he told me in therapy. During adolescence, Eric would protest about the quiet dinners, because he liked to discuss matters of current interest, but his father's belt, which he pulled out like a whip, quickly put Eric in his place.

Eric's mother was involved in an affair from the time he was 13 until he was 18. The father did not confront her, but Eric did after he finished high school. The affair stopped after his confrontation. In retrospect, he felt that his mother was more dependent upon him than on her husband, and Eric looked out for her.

In Michelle's home she was never complimented on her looks or her excellence in academic performance by her mother. She was the oldest of four children and played surrogate mother to her siblings, as her mother was ill quite often. Although Michelle did a great deal of housework, cooking, and cleaning, she was viewed by her mother as not being good enough in taking care of her siblings or excelling in school. Her father was more supportive whenever he was available. Michelle remembers going out on her prom night after spending hours in front of the mirror. She wore a beautiful, pale pink, long dress, which she thought was very becoming of her, but her mother looked at her and said, "Michelle, you look pale, and dull. I'm sure others have dressed up better than you." Michelle was crushed. She said that her mother was very critical of her and very good at finding faults.

Michelle and Eric made an interesting pair. Eric liked taking care of women, like his mother, in a controlling manner, and Michelle was dependent, diffident, and looked for approval as she did growing up at home. From the outside, both Eric and Michelle appeared to be very sensitive but as I entered their home life, their lack of intimacy was very obvious. Quite often in the marriage, Eric treated her like a student. Their money was separate; they had separate accounts and one joint account in which they put money for groceries. If they ate out together, which they did quite often (*only* at Eric's favorite restaurants), each one had to pay for himself or herself. In case Eric paid for Michelle, he would take that money out of the joint account as his own money. They used separate bathrooms in the house, and when Michelle ran out of toilet paper and Eric had to buy it he would charge her for it or leave the receipt for reimbursement on the kitchen table. Michelle said that in her earlier marriage she took care of all the money but it was different in this marriage. In individual sessions, she complained that he had changed a great deal after their marriage. He had been a caring, loving confidante with whom she could share all her secrets and problems prior to the marriage, but they had literally become strangers in the house. Michelle lamented that Eric was aloof. It seemed to me that in a legal and intimate relationship he had to draw lines to protect himself, or perhaps this was his notion of family life, as he had experienced an earlier home life where feelings and intimacy were looked down upon.

An incident in their marriage opened up more clues about their relationship. Eric maintained a journal in which he had written every day for twenty years. As Eric became more and more closed up in the marriage, Michelle became suspicious. Michelle opened his journal and read it without his permission, later confessing about it. In the joint session that followed this incident, Eric called her names because she was unworthy and untrusting, and the names he used included "motel whore," "tramp," and the like. In this session, Michelle quickly took the one-down position and cried, which she did a great deal. My attempts to empower her were fruitless. At this point I asked them what they wanted out of the marriage. Both of them were angry with each other but also insecure in love, and both wanted to work at the marriage. I asked Eric why he had closed up to Michelle. Eric responded that when they had fights, which was quite often, Michelle would talk negatively about his family and Michelle retorted that he did the same with hers. At one point, when they were in bed and fighting, Michelle got out of the bed in the nude and ran out of the front door and got into her car. Eric panicked because he was afraid that she would get into an accident or be arrested. Fortunately, she returned back home in ten minutes and nothing worse happened. However, this behavior shocked him. She retorted that he was very critical of her and she had felt overwhelmed by his attitude, and that was the reason for running to her car. She realized that it was not acceptable behavior and would not do it again. She sighed and added that this incident had happened four years ago and she wished that Eric would forget it. When they fought, Michelle would find a place in her study, or a corner in the kitchen in *his house*, and sleep on the floor by herself. If she dared to sleep anywhere else, like on the living room couch, he would be angry, as she had "no permission to do so." It was *his* house. I experienced both of them as very separate, as if living in separate cages in a pet store.

In therapy, intimacy was seen as the key problem. Eric would be very friendly, helpful, and warm with people who were outsiders whom he could help, but once they became part of his personal life he would quickly move away and play the role of a superior person, particularly intellectually, as he was the teacher and professor of all his girlfriends. He also confessed that in his relationships with people he tended to withdraw once they became intimate. He added thoughtfully that his tears, fears, and shame were always laughed at at home while growing up, and therefore he learned to be in control of all his feelings. In his relationships he felt that showing feelings meant being vulnerable.

Michelle came from a home where nothing she did was good enough, and where her mother had been very critical of her capabilities and her looks. Michelle carried this sense of defeat and inferiority into her relationships. To help this couple become intimate was a challenge. I alternated them between individual and couple sessions. After each one had worked at developing a clear awareness of their own sense of self, they were given exercises or tasks to perform. This included Eric "allowing" Michelle to decorate the kitchen and the rest of the house, except his study, with some of her things. Michelle had to do this without asking for his permission. Diffident and hesitant, Michelle started to redecorate the house and eventually started to enjoy it. Although Eric was reluctant in the initial stages, he began to like what Michelle did, and said so in the couple sessions. Eric learned to give compliments, and Michelle learned to give and take compliments without feeling diffident. Other task assignments included holding hands and talking to each other, focusing on noncontroversial topics that could not upset either one of them. Eric began to introduce his own friends to Michelle and she did the same. They planned fun outings and started to enjoy each other. At one point, I asked Michelle to share her work ideas (she was an interior decorator) for the antique shop that he had opened as a new business, after he gave up teaching as a career. (He mentioned that academia was too political for him!) Although hesitant as usual, he agreed and was pleased with her ideas. Gradually, Eric helped her to open up her own small part-time business (besides her full-time job) in his shop, where she could sell her interior decoration ideas, and did not charge her (!) for the space.

Their joint account became bigger, and they pooled more and more of their money and budgeted everything jointly. Michelle opened up and talked to him about her younger daughter, Suzi, whom Eric had liked but distanced himself from after the marriage. She was visiting them from college and Michelle generously mentioned that he could plan to spend some separate time with her if he wanted to. Eric was surprised and seeing "no catches" in this situation agreed to do so. Both were intellectuals and enjoyed books, and this soon became an intimate part of their lives where they discussed topics of interest. Eric had avoided verbally telling Michelle that he loved her soon after their marriage. She complained that she would consider herself lucky if he said so more than once a year. They had been married for over six years. This was a power and control game for Eric. He knew what it felt like to not hear affectionate terms while growing up, and in his marriage he used it against Michelle when he found out that this was what she would like to hear. When he realized that matters would get better between them, and that it was good for him as well, he started to verbalize his love by saying that he loved her more often, and she did the same. The ground rule was that each one could not use the other's weaknesses or vulnerabilities when they fought about anything, big or small. It took a number of sessions before they began to work together intimately without throwing negatives at each other.

Confiding in each other, which had taken a bad turn in their marriage, was rebuilt through task assignments and talks between them. Toward the end of therapy, Eric mentioned that the ownership of the house *just by him* had caused them tremendous grief and therefore, at the right time, they sold his house and bought one together. A great deal of sophistication came through in caring, sharing, and vulnerability in therapy, and the best statement I heard from Eric was "I'm not the marrying type, but in spite of myself, I made the right choice in marrying Michelle." Michelle learned to be less diffident in their relationship, and worked hard at not playing the one-down position or the student role. The most helpful technique with her was to help her have down-to-earth discussions about home, work, and planning for the future with Eric where she could stand on her own. This led to developing self-confidence and, with Eric's emotional support and overt expression of love, she blossomed.

Taking over the household and creating a new home, with her ideas being appreciated, was another positive addition to her sense of self. Eric recognized his rigidity and worked hard at breaking down the barriers that interfered with his marriage. The sessions were less frequent as they came together more and more as mutual partners with love and respect. Most of their ability to be intimate started with understanding their own family history and diligently carrying out the task assignments, and it eventually led to openness, vulnerability and true intimacy. I am sure that they probably still have some ups and downs, but this would not affect the strength that they saw and developed in their relationship. There was a conscious effort on both their parts to break down the barriers they had developed earlier in their lives. Eric said that "we" was really and truly better than "I" and Michelle added that "I" is a lonely word.

To work through life's issues, irrespective of the problems that a person has faced, is to learn to communicate, to be aware, to work on one's boundaries, and to begin intimacy. Being intimate with a person requires mutual risk. If there is a one-way relationship, where only you believe you are intimate, this can shame you and cause you to develop deeper patterns of dependency. Conversely, when you attempt to share your deepest thoughts and feelings and this is rebuffed by your partner, you are bound to feel hurt. In that case, it would probably be best to wait for a period of time and try again on a slightly less intimate, less threatening level.

Finally, growth is a life-long process. Everyone, given a chance and the right atmosphere, will begin to blossom. However, like different flowers, each one of us, depending upon the rain our roots have received in our families of origin, will blossom at different levels and at different points. Often this whole process can be accelerated with an awareness of the need for help.

References

Ainsworth, S., Blehar, M. C., Waters, E., and Wall, S. (1978). *Patterns of Attachment.* Hillsdale, NJ: Erlbaum.

Allen, M. (1993). *Angry Men, Passive Men*. New York: Fawcett Columbia.

Beavers, W. R. (1995). *Successful Marriage*. New York: Norton and Norton.

Beck, A. T. (1989). *Love is Not Enough*. New York: Harper Perennial.

Boszormenyi-Nagy, I., and Krasner, B. R. (1986). *Between Give and Take*. New York: Brunner/Mazel.

Boszormenyi-Nagy, I., and Spark, G. M., (1984). *Invisible Loyalties*. New York: Brunner/Mazel.

Bowlby, J. (1973). *Attachment and Loss. Vol. 2, Separation*. New York: Basic Books.

Bradshaw, J. (1988). *The Family*. Deerfield Beach, FL: Health Communications.

Byng-Hall, J. (1973). Family myths used as defense in conjoint family therapy. *British Journal of Medical Psychology* 46:239–250.

——— (1988). Scripts and legends in families and family therapy. *Family Process* 27:167–179.

Carlson, D. L. (1981). *Overcoming Hurts and Anger*. Eugene, OR: Harvest House.

Cutler, W. B., Garcia, C. R., and McCoy, N. L. (1987). Perimenopausal sexuality. *Archives of Sexual Behavior* 16:225–234.

DeLameter, J. D., and MacCorquodale, P. (1973). *Premarital Sexuality: Attitudes, Relationships, Behavior*. Madison, WI: University of Wisconsin Press.

Elliott, G. R., and Eisdorfer, C., eds. (1982). *Stress and Human Health*. New York: Springer.

Ellis, A. (1977). *How to Live with and without Anger*. New York: Reader's Digest Press.

Erikson, E. (1963). *Childhood and Society*. New York: Norton and Norton.

Fehr, B. (1988). Prototype analysis of the concept of love and commitment. *Journal of Personality and Social Psychology* 55:557–579.

Forward, S. (1989). *Toxic Parents*. New York: Bantam.

Fossum, M., and Mason, M. (1986). *Facing Shame: Families in Recovery*. New York: Norton. Cited in *Secrets in Families and Family Therapy*, ed. E. Imber-Black (1993). New York: Norton.

Foster, C. (1993). *The Family Patterns Workbook*. New York: Putnam.

Gadpaille, W. J. (1975). *The Cycles of Sex*. New York: Scribner's.

Goleman, D. (1987). Shame steps out of hiding and into sharper focus. *New York Times*, September 15, p. 23.

Goodman, G., and Esterly, G. (1988). *The Talk Book*. New York: Ballantine.

Goodwin, D. W. (1986). *Anxiety*. New York: Ballantine.

Gray, J. (1984). *What You Feel You Can Heal*. Mill Valley, CA: Heart Publishing.

——— (1992). *Men Are from Mars, Women Are from Venus*. New York: HarperCollins.

Haley, J. (1963). *Strategies of Psychotherapy*. New York: Grune & Stratton.

Imber-Black, E., ed. (1993). *Secrets in Families and Family Therapy*. New York: Norton.

Kerr, M. E., and Bowen, M. (1988). *Family Evaluation: An Approach Based on Bowen Theory*. New York: Norton and Norton.

Lerner, H. G. (1989). *The Dance of Intimacy*. New York: Harper & Row.

Lew, M. (1988). *Victims No Longer*. New York: Harper & Row.

Lively, V., and Lively, E. (1991). *Sexual Development of Young Children*. Albany, NY: Demar.

Maltz, D., and Borker, R. (1982). Cognitive-behavioral treatment of remarried families. In *Cognitive-Behavioral Therapy with Families*, ed. J. J. Gumper, Cambridge, UK: Cambridge University Press.

Maltz, W., and Holman, B. (1987). *Incest and Sexuality*. Lexington, MA: Lexington Books.

Marshall, D. (1971). Sexual behavior in Mangaia. In *Human Sexual Behavior*, ed. D. Marshall and R. Suggs, pp. 103–162. New York: Basic Books.

Martin, T. C., and Bumpass, L. L. (1989). Recent trends in marital disruption. *Demography* 26:37–51.

Martinson, F. M. (1981). Eroticism in infancy and childhood. In *Children and Sex: New Findings, New Perspectives*, ed. L. L. Constantine and F. M. Martinson, pp. 23–35. Boston: Little, Brown.

Mason, M. (1986). Shame: reservoir of secrets. In *Secrets in Families and Family Therapy,* ed. E. Imber-Black, pp. 29–43. New York: Norton.

Masters, W. H., Johnson, V. E., and Kolodny, R. C. (1988). *On Sex and Human Loving*. Boston: Little, Brown.

Menaghan, E. G. (1995). Stress. In *Encyclopedia of Marriage and the Family*, vol. 2, ed. D. Levinson, pp. 686–692. New York: Simon & Schuster.

Money, J. (1980). *Love and Love Sickness*. Baltimore: Johns Hopkins University Press.

O'Neill, E. (1971). *The Iceman Cometh*. Harmondsworth, NY: Penguin.

Paine-Gernee, K., and Hunt, I. (1990). *Emotional Healing: A Program for Emotional Sobriety*. New York: Warner.

Pearlin, L. I. (1989). The sociological study of stress. *Journal of Health and Social Behavior* 30:241–256.

Pearlin, L. I., Lieberman, M. A., Menaghan, E. G., and Mullen, J. I. (1981). The stress process. *Journal of Health and Social Behavior* 22:337–356.

Pillari, V. (1986). *Pathways to Family Myths*. New York: Brunner/Mazel.

——— (1991). *Scapegoating in Families*. New York: Brunner/Mazel.

——— (1994). *Family Myths in Therapy*. Northvale, NJ: Jason Aronson.

Pittman, F. (1989). *Private Lies*. New York: Ballantine.

Prager, K. J. (1995). Intimacy. In *Encyclopedia of Marriage and the Family*, Vol. 2, ed. D. Levinson, pp. 402–407. New York: Simon & Schuster.

Reinisch, J. (1990). *The Kinsey Report on Sex*. New York: St. Martin's.

Rempel, J. K. (1995). Trust. In *Encyclopedia of Marriage and the Family*, ed. D. Levinson, pp. 725–729. New York: Simon & Schuster.

Roskies, E. (1991). Stress management: a new approach. In *Stress and Coping*, ed. A. Monat and R. S. Lazarus, pp. 407–431. New York: Columbia University Press.

Satir, V. M. (1982). The therapist and family therapy: process model. In *Family Counseling and Therapy*, ed. A. M. Horner and M. M. Ohlsen, Itasca, IL: Peacock.

Satir, V. M., and Baldwin, M. (1983). *Satir Step by Step: A Guide to Creating Change in Families*. Palo Alto, CA: Science and Behavioral Books.

Schwartz, R. (1985). *Family of origin: a journey home again*. Paper presented at Family Therapy Institute, 15th anniversary, St. Paul, MN.

Selye, H. (1991). History and present status of the stress concept. In *Stress and Coping*, ed. A. Monat and R. S. Lazarus, pp. 21–35. New York: Columbia University Press.

Sheldon, R. (1982). *Relationships*. Virginia Beach, VA: Creative Communications Co.

Smith, T. W. (1991). Adult sexual behavior in 1989: number of partners, frequency of intercourse and risk of AIDS. *Family Planning Perspectives* 23:102–107.

Visher, E. B., and Visher, J. S. (1988). *Old Loyalties and New Ties*. New York: Brunner/Mazel.

Whitfield, C. L. (1993). *Boundaries and Relationships*. Deerfield Beach, FL: Health Communications.

Wiederman, M. W. (1995). Sexuality in the life cycle. In *The Encyclopedia of Marriage and the Family*, ed. D. Levinson, pp. 362–368. New York: Macmillan.

Winn, R. L., and Newton, N. (1982). Sexuality in aging: a study of 106 cultures. *Archives of Sexual Behavior* 11:283–298.

Wynne, L. (1961). The study of intrafamilial alignments and splits in exploratory family therapy. In *Exploring the Base for Family Therapy*, ed. N. W. Ackerman, F. L. Beatman, and S. N. Sherman. New York: Family Service Association of America.

Wynne, L., Ryckoff, I., Day, J., and Hirsch, S. (1958). Pseudomutuality in the family relations of schizophrenics. *Psychiatry* 21:205–220.

Wynne, L. C., and Wynne, A. R. (1986). The quest of intimacy. *Journal of Marital and Family Therapy* 12:383–393.

Index